Zero heroes

Seven C3

Produced by Seven Publishing Ltd on behalf of WW International, Inc. Published June 2020. All rights reserved. No part of this publication may be reproduced, stored in a retrieval system or transmitted in any form by any means, electronic, mechanical photocopying, recording or otherwise, without the prior written permission of Seven Publishing Ltd. First published in Great Britain by Seven Publishing Ltd.

Seven Publishing Ltd
3-7 Herbal Hill
London EC1R 5EJ
seven.co.uk

A CIP catalogue record for this book is available from the British Library.

ISBN: 978-1-9996673-9-9

WW PUBLICATIONS TEAM
Samantha Rees, Harriet Joy, Jessica O'Shea, Nicola Kirk
With thanks to: Shelley Fletcher

FOR SEVEN PUBLISHING LTD
Editorial
Editor-in-Chief: Helen Renshaw
Editor: Christine Faughlin
Sub-editor: Ward Hellewell

FOOD
Recipes Cate Dixon, Anita Janusic, Lucy Jessop, Hannah Yeadon

DESIGN & PHOTOGRAPHY
Art director: Liz Baird
Photography: Luke J Albert
Food styling: Emily Kydd, Jenna Leiter
Prop styling: Olivia Wardle
Additional photography:
WW Global Asset Bank

ACCOUNT MANAGEMENT
Senior account manager:
Gina Cavaciuti
Group publishing director:
Kirsten Price

PRODUCTION
Print lead: Liz Knipe
Colour reproduction by F1 Colour
Printed in the UK by CPI Colour

Contents

6   Introduction

8   About our recipes

10 ZeroPoint foods guide

18 Fruit & veg

46 Fish & poultry

70 Pulses & grains

88 Eggs & dairy

102 Quorn & tofu

118 Meal plans

126 Indexes

Start at zero

Cooking healthy meals for yourself and those you love is so much easier when you start with 'zero heroes' – ingredients you'll find on the ZeroPoint foods list. They have a SmartPoints® value of zero, so don't need to be tracked, measured or weighed – and that's precisely why they're great foods to build on when whipping up a meal, or turn to when reaching for a snack. The versatile recipes in this book are designed to help you experiment with the zero heroes you're already familiar with, and explore some you might not have tried yet. With more than 60 recipe ideas for breakfasts, lunches, dinners, puds and snacks, you'll find lots of inspo you can come back to time and time again. Enjoy!

About our recipes

Our cookbooks are packed with recipes that are both nutritious and delicious...

Our recipes are designed to encourage a healthier way of eating with lots of ZeroPoint foods and lower SmartPoints value ingredients to make the most of your Budget. Here's how to better understand our recipes and the ingredients that go into them:

Ingredients

EGGS We use medium eggs, unless otherwise stated. Pregnant women, the elderly and children should avoid recipes with eggs which are raw or not fully cooked if not produced under the British Lion code of practice.

FRUIT AND VEGETABLES Recipes use medium-size fruit and veg, unless otherwise stated.

LOW-FAT SPREAD When a recipe uses a low-fat spread, we mean a spread with a fat content of no more than 39 per cent.

REDUCED-FAT SOFT CHEESE Where a recipe uses medium-fat soft cheese, we mean a soft cheese with 30 per cent less fat than its full-fat equivalent; where a recipe uses low-fat soft cheese, we mean a soft cheese with 5 per cent fat.

Prepping and cooking

PREP AND COOK TIMES These are approximate and meant to be guidelines only. Prep time includes all steps up to and following the main cooking time(s). Stated cook times may vary according to your oven.

MICROWAVES If we've used a microwave in any of our recipes, the timings will be for an 850-watt microwave oven.

Dietary requirements

VEGETARIAN RECIPES Recipes displaying a vegetarian symbol include non-meat ingredients, but may also contain processed products that aren't always vegetarian, such as pesto. If you're a vegetarian, you should ensure you use vegetarian varieties and check the ingredients labels. Where we reference vegetarian Italian-style hard cheese in vegetarian recipes, we mean a cheese similar to Parmesan (which is not vegetarian) but which is suitable for vegetarians.

VEGAN RECIPES Recipes displaying a vegan symbol include no products made from or with the aid of animals or animal products.

GLUTEN-FREE RECIPES Recipes that are labelled as gluten free include ingredients that naturally do not contain gluten, but they may also contain processed products, such as sauces, stock cubes and spice mixes. If so, you should ensure that those products do not include any gluten-containing ingredients (wheat, barley or rye) – these will be highlighted in the ingredients list on the product label. Manufacturers may also indicate whether there is a chance their product may have been accidentally contaminated with gluten during the manufacturing process. For more information and guidance on gluten-free products, visit www.coeliac.org.uk

NUT-FREE RECIPES Recipes displaying a nut free symbol include ingredients that do not contain nuts and/or certain seeds, but may include ingredients produced in facilities that also handle nut or seed products. If you have a nut or seed allergy, check over the ingredients labels for more information.

DAIRY-FREE RECIPES Recipes displaying a dairy free symbol include ingredients that naturally do not contain dairy, but may include ingredients produced in facilities that also handle dairy products. If you have a dairy allergy, check ingredients labels for more information.

SmartPoints calculations

SmartPoints values for the recipes in this book are calculated using the values for generic foods, not brands (except where stated). Tracking using branded items may affect the recorded SmartPoints.

WHEN YOU SEE THESE SYMBOLS:

Tells you the SmartPoints value per serving for each plan.

Note: Recipes conform to the icon designations, but tip and serving suggestions may not.

 Indicates a recipe is gluten free

 Indicates a recipe is vegetarian

 Indicates a recipe is vegan

 Indicates a recipe is nut free

 Indicates a recipe is dairy free

Zero heroes make eating simpler

Want to know the secret to successful healthy eating? Incorporating as many ingredients from your ZeroPoint foods list as possible into your day.

As you know, all foods have a SmartPoints value. But lots are ZeroPoint foods, which are exactly what they sound like – foods that have a zero SmartPoints value. These foods are healthy, easy to get hold of and form the basis of healthy eating. You can enjoy them without weighing, measuring or tracking so they add flexibility to your SmartPoints Budget – across Green, Blue and Purple.

Can I eat as many zero heroes as I like?

While there's no need to measure or track ZeroPoint foods, that's not to say they're an all-you-can-eat option. Eating any food – even ZeroPoint foods – excessively could lead to weight gain. A simple approach is to eat them until comfortably full.

Should I aim to only eat ZeroPoint foods?

As great as they are, the aim is to not just eat ZeroPoint foods. You might have a favourite zero hero (who doesn't love butternut squash!) and that's okay, but limiting yourself to certain foods is a recipe for boredom.

Will I have to buy lots of special ingredients?

Not at all – ZeroPoint foods are regular, everyday foods that are easy to get hold of. Whether you're using them for snacks, as the starting point for all your meals, or to add variety to your favourite recipes, you're unlikely to be eating differently from your family and friends.

Where should I start?

Our ZeroPoint foods list for Green, Blue and Purple include most fruit and vegetables. If you're on Blue or Purple, you'll also find plenty of lean proteins, pulses and dairy options on your list. Aim to use at least one of these as the base of most of your meals, and then build recipes around it using added extras.

You could, for example, whip up a delicious recipe based on ZeroPoint foods, and then spend your remaining SmartPoints Budget on side dishes, desserts, or snacks across the day.

Or, you could lean on ZeroPoint foods to create meals that are a little more indulgent than usual. For example, making a meal with zero hero ingredients at its core, and then using your SmartPoints Budget for those added extras that can make a meal special. So if you want to sprinkle grated Parmesan cheese on your pasta, or serve a crusty roll alongside your soup, you can.

Turn the page for sample lists of many of the ZeroPoint foods you'll find on Green, Blue and Purple, and then discover how to use them to their best advantage in more than 60 delicious, inspirational recipes from page 18 onwards.

Green

Green guides you towards a smaller list of foods that form the basis of healthy eating habits, with a sizeable SmartPoints Budget to spend on other foods. You'll build meals and snacks around 100+ ZeroPoint foods including fruits and non-starchy veg, and track other foods that have SmartPoints values.

Blue

Blue guides you towards a list of foods that form the basis of healthy eating habits, with a moderate SmartPoints Budget you can spend on other foods you love. You'll build meals around 200+ ZeroPoint foods including fruit, veg, eggs, skinless chicken and turkey breast, fish and shellfish, fat-free yogurt and soya yogurt, beans and legumes, and tofu, Quorn and tempeh, and track other foods that have SmartPoints values.

Purple

Purple guides you towards a long list of foods that form the basis of healthy eating habits, with a modest SmartPoints Budget that you can spend on other foods you love. You'll build meals around 300+ ZeroPoint foods including fruit, veg, eggs, skinless chicken and turkey breast, fish and shellfish, fat-free yogurt and soya yogurt, beans and legumes, tofu, Quorn and tempeh, wholewheat pasta and grains, and potatoes, and track other foods that have SmartPoints values.

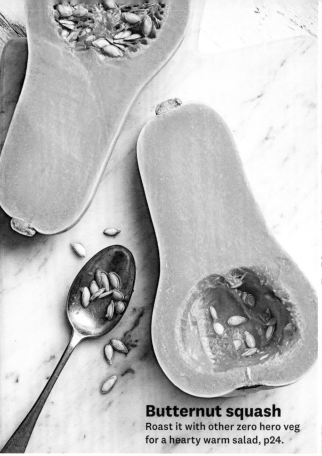

Butternut squash
Roast it with other zero hero veg for a hearty warm salad, p24.

Tomatoes
Fresh or tinned, tomatoes are a good base for lots of meals. Cook them with harissa to make a tasty sauce, p68.

Green: Your ZeroPoint foods list

You can enjoy more than 100 fresh fruits and non-starchy vegetables – mix and match them with all your favourite foods, without having to focus on measuring, weighing or tracking them.

Find a full version of the ZeroPoint foods list on the WW website or the WW app

FRUITS

Apples
Apricots (fresh)
Bananas
Blackberries
Blueberries
Cantaloupe melons
Cherries
Clementines
Cranberries (fresh)
Dragon fruits
Figs (fresh)
Frozen mixed berries (unsweetened)
Fruit cocktail (unsweetened)
Grapefruits
Grapes
Guava
Honeydew melons
Kiwi fruits
Kumquats
Lemons
Limes
Mangoes
Nectarines
Oranges
Papayas
Peaches
Pears
Persimmons
Pineapples
Plums
Pomegranates
Pomelo
Raspberries
Star fruit
Strawberries
Tangerines
Watermelons

VEGETABLES (NON-STARCHY) & HERBS

Acorn squash
Artichoke hearts (no oil)
Artichokes
Asparagus
Aubergines
Baby corn
Basil
Beetroot
Broccoli
Brussels sprouts
Butternut squash
Cabbage
Carrots
Cauliflower
Cauliflower rice
Celery
Chives
Coriander
Courgettes
Cucumber
Endive
Fennel
Frozen stir-fry vegetables (no sauce)
Garlic
Ginger
Green beans
Kale
Kohlrabi
Leeks
Lettuce (all types)
Mint
Mixed greens
Mushrooms
Nori (seaweed)
Okra
Onions
Oregano
Pak choi
Parsley
Pea shoots
Peppers
Pickles (unsweetened)
Pumpkin
Radishes
Rocket
Rosemary
Shallots
Spaghetti squash
Spinach
Spring onions
Swiss chard
Tarragon
Thyme
Tomatoes
Turnips
Water chestnuts

Blue: Your ZeroPoint foods list

You can call on more than 200 zero heroes, including most fruits, non-starchy vegetables, eggs, skinless chicken and turkey breast fillets, fish and shellfish, beans and legumes, tofu and tempeh, and fat-free plain yogurt.

BEANS & LEGUMES
Black beans
Black-eyed peas
Cannellini beans
Chickpeas
Kidney beans
Lentils
Lima beans
Pinto beans
Refried beans
(fat-free, tinned)
Soya beans

CHICKEN & TURKEY BREAST
Chicken breast mince
Skinless chicken breast fillets
Skinless turkey breast fillets
Turkey breast mince

EGGS
Eggs, all types

FAT-FREE YOGURT & SOYA
Greek yogurt
(plain, fat-free)
Plain yogurt
(fat-free)
Quark
(plain, fat-free)
Soya yogurt
(plain)

FISH & SHELLFISH
Anchovies
(in water)
Carp
Catfish
Caviar
Clams
Cod
Crabmeat (lump)
Crayfish
Cuttlefish
Eel
Fish roe
Flounder
Grouper
Haddock
Halibut
Herring
Lobster
Mahi mahi
Monkfish
Mussels
Octopus
Orange roughy
Oysters
Perch
Pike
Pollock
Pompano
Prawns
Salmon
Sardines (tinned, in water or brine)
Sashimi
Scallops
Sea bass
Sea cucumber
Sea urchin
Shrimp
Smoked haddock
Smoked mackerel
Smoked salmon
Smoked sturgeon
Smoked trout
Smoked whitefish
Snapper
Sole
Squid
Sturgeon
Swordfish
Tilapia
Trout
Tuna
Turbot
White fish

FRUITS
Apples
Apricots (fresh)
Bananas
Blackberries
Blueberries
Cantaloupe melons
Cherries
Clementines
Cranberries
(fresh)
Dragon fruits
Figs (fresh)
Frozen mixed berries
(unsweetened)
Fruit cocktail
(unsweetened)
Grapefruits
Grapes
Guava
Honeydew melons
Kiwi fruits
Kumquats
Lemons
Limes
Mangoes
Nectarines
Oranges
Papayas
Peaches
Pears
Persimmons
Pineapples
Plums
Pomegranates
Pomelo
Raspberries
Star fruit
Strawberries
Tangerines
Watermelons

QUORN, TOFU AND TEMPEH
Quorn
(plain, all types)
Tempeh
(plain, all types)
Tofu (plain, all types)

VEGETABLES (NON-STARCHY) & HERBS
Acorn squash
Artichoke hearts
(no oil)
Artichokes
Asparagus
Aubergines
Baby corn
Bamboo shoots
Basil
Bean sprouts
Beetroot
Broad beans
Broccoli
Brussels sprouts
Butternut squash
Cabbage
(all types)
Carrots
Cauliflower
Cauliflower rice
Celery
Chives
Coriander
Corn on the cob
Courgettes
Cucumber
Edamame
Endive
Fennel
Garlic
Ginger
Green beans
Kale
Kohlrabi
Leeks
Lettuce
(all types)
Mint
Mixed greens
Mushrooms
Nori (seaweed)
Okra
Onions
Oregano
Pak choi
Parsley
Parsnips
Peas
Pea shoots
Peppers
Pickles
(unsweetened)
Pumpkin
Radishes
Rocket
Rosemary
Shallots
Spring onions
Spaghetti squash
Spinach
Sweetcorn
Swiss chard
Tarragon
Thyme
Tomatoes
Turnips
Water chestnuts

Find a full version of the ZeroPoint foods list on the WW website or the WW app

Purple: Your ZeroPoint foods list

There are more than 300 zero heroes to turn to, including everything you'll find on the Green and Blue lists, as well as potatoes, wholewheat pasta and grains, and more.

BEANS & LEGUMES
Aduki beans
Black bean pasta
Black beans
Black-eyed peas
Cannellini beans
Chickpea pasta
Chickpeas
Kidney beans
Lentil pasta
Lentils
Lima beans
Pea pasta
Pinto beans
Refried beans (tinned, fat-free)
Soya beans
Soybean pasta
Split peas

CHICKEN & TURKEY BREAST
Chicken breast mince
Skinless chicken breast fillets
Skinless turkey breast fillets
Turkey breast mince

EGGS
Eggs (all types)

FAT-FREE YOGURT & SOYA
Cottage cheese (plain, fat-free)
Greek yogurt (plain, fat-free)
Plain yogurt (fat-free)
Quark (plain, fat-free)
Soya yogurt (plain)

FISH & SHELLFISH
Abalone
Anchovies
Carp
Catfish
Caviar
Clams
Cod
Crabmeat (lump)
Crayfish
Cuttlefish
Eel
Fish roe
Flounder
Grouper
Haddock
Halibut
Herring
Hominy
Lobster
Mahi mahi
Monkfish
Mussels

Octopus
Orange roughy
Oysters
Perch
Pike
Pollock
Prawns
Salmon
Sardines (tinned, in water or brine)
Sashimi
Scallops
Sea bass
Sea cucumber
Sea urchin
Shrimp
Smelt
Smoked haddock
Smoked mackerel
Smoked salmon
Smoked sturgeon
Smoked trout
Smoked whitefish
Snapper
Sole
Squid
Sturgeon
Swordfish
Tilapia
Trout
Tuna
Tuna (tinned, in water or brine)
Turbot
Whitefish

FRUITS
Apples
Apricots (fresh)
Bananas
Blackberries
Blueberries
Cantaloupe melons
Cherries
Clementines
Cranberries (fresh)
Dragon fruits
Figs (fresh)
Frozen mixed berries, (unsweetened)
Fruit cocktail (unsweetened)
Grapefruit
Grapes
Guava
Honeydew melons
Kiwi fruits
Kumquats
Lemons
Limes
Mangoes
Nectarines
Oranges
Papayas
Peaches
Pears
Persimmons
Pineapples
Plums
Pomegranates

Pomelo
Raspberries
Star fruit
Strawberries
Tangerines
Watermelon

PASTA, RICE & GRAINS
Amaranth
Barley
Brown basmati rice
Brown rice
Brown rice noodles
Brown rice pasta
Brown rice quinoa blend
Buckwheat
Bulgur wheat
Edamame pasta
Farro
Freekeh
Kamut
Kasha
Millet
Oats
Popcorn (air-popped, plain, made without oil)
Popcorn kernels (plain)
Quinoa
Quinoa pasta
Red quinoa
Rolled oats
Rye
Soba noodles, (100% buckwheat)
Sorghum
Spelt
Spelt berries
Teff
Thai brown rice
Tricolour quinoa
Wheatberries
Wholewheat couscous
Wholewheat pasta
Wholewheat sorghum
Wild rice

Wild rice (brown)

QUORN, TOFU AND TEMPEH
Quorn (plain, all types)
Silken tofu
Smoked tofu
Tempeh (plain, all types)
Tofu (plain, all types)

VEGETABLES (NON-STARCHY) & HERBS
Acorn squash
Alfalfa sprouts
Artichoke hearts (no oil)
Artichokes
Asparagus
Baby corn
Bamboo shoots
Basil
Beansprouts
Beetroot
Broad beans
Broccoli
Brussels sprouts
Butternut squash
Cabbage (all types)
Carrots
Cauliflower
Cauliflower rice
Celery
Chives
Coriander
Courgettes
Cucumber
Edamame
Endive
Fennel
Frozen stir-fry vegetables (no sauce)
Garlic
Ginger
Green beans
Kale
Kohlrabi
Leeks
Lettuce (all types)

Mint
Mixed greens
Mushrooms
Nori (seaweed)
Okra
Onions
Oregano
Parsley
Parsnips
Peas
Pea shoots
Peppers
Pickles (unsweetened)
Pumpkin
Radishes
Rosemary
Salsa (fresh, no oil)
Sauerkraut
Shallots
Spaghetti squash
Spinach
Spring onions
Swiss chard
Tarragon
Thyme
Tomatoes
Turnips
Water chestnuts

VEGETABLES (STARCHY)
Baby potatoes
Cassava
Corn
Corn (tinned)
Mashed potatoes (plain)
Mashed sweet potatoes (plain)
New potatoes
Potatoes
Sweet potatoes
Taro
Yams
Yuca

Find a full version of the ZeroPoint foods list on the WW website or the WW app

Fruit & veg

20 **Apple & oat crisp**
Apple & ginger overnight oats
Toffee & walnut baked apples
Apple & kale slaw

22 **Spiced courgette soup**

24 **Roasted Tenderstem broccoli salad with cashew dressing**

26 **Spiced squash & cauliflower fritters with red pepper salsa**

28 **Red cabbage slaw**

30 **Roast beetroot burgers**

32 **Cauliflower 'risotto'**

34 **Griddled lettuce with red pepper pesto & chimichurri**

36 **Satay vegetable noodles**

38 **Fruit salad with lime dressing**

40 **Plum & pistachio crumble**

42 **Pineapple waffles**

44 **Spice-roasted vegetables**
Roasted beetroot houmous
Celeriac soup with ricotta toast
Rosemary swede chips

Four variations... **Apples**

Cored and baked whole with walnuts, grated raw into muesli and slaw, or stewed in a crumble with cinnamon – apples are the everyday fruit that always delivers.

Apple & oat crisp

serves 4   **prep time 10 minutes**   **cook time 35 minutes**

  per serving

Preheat the oven to 200°C, fan 180°C, gas mark 6. Peel, core and chop 6 **Gala apples** into 2cm pieces and put into a large pan with 60ml **cloudy apple juice**, 40ml water and 1½ teaspoons **ground cinnamon**. Cover and bring to the boil, then reduce the heat and simmer for 10-15 minutes, stirring occasionally, until the apples have started to break down and the liquid has almost evaporated. Tip the apples into a small baking dish. Melt 1 tablespoon **coconut oil** in a small pan over a medium heat, then stir in 30g **porridge oats**. Scatter the oat mixture and 20g chopped **dark chocolate** over the fruit, and bake for 20 minutes until the oats are golden and the chocolate has melted.

Apple & ginger overnight oats

serves 1   **prep time 10 minutes + soaking**

  per serving

The night before you want to serve the oats, mix together 30g **porridge oats**, 80ml **unsweetened almond drink** and ½ teaspoon **ground ginger** in a Kilner jar or bowl. Cover and chill in the fridge overnight. The next morning, loosen the oats with a splash of water, if needed. Grate ¼ **Braeburn apple** and mix through the oats, then finely chop another ¼ apple and scatter over the oats along with 4 halved **raspberries**. Combine 1½ tablespoons **PBFit Peanut Butter Powder** with 1 tablespoon water until smooth, then spoon the mixture over the oats and serve.

Toffee & walnut baked apples

serves 4   **prep time 15 minutes**   **cook time 50 minutes**

  per serving

Preheat the oven to 180°C, fan 160°C, gas mark 4. Put 20g chopped **walnuts**, 20g **dark muscovado sugar** and ½ teaspoon **ground cinnamon** in a bowl. Prick 4 cored **Braeburn apples** all over with a fork, add them to the bowl and mix together until well combined. Sit the cored apples in a small baking dish, just big enough to hold them. Fill the holes with the walnut mixture and bake for 30 minutes, until the apples are soft. Meanwhile, put 25g **plain flour**, 1 teaspoon **ground cinnamon** and 15g melted **low-fat spread** in a mixing bowl then use your fingertips to rub everything together until the mixture clumps. Stir in 10g dark muscovado sugar, then scatter the mixture over the tops of the apples. Bake for a further 20 minutes until golden.

Apple & kale slaw

serves 4   **prep time 20 minutes**   **cook time 5 minutes**

  per serving

Toast 1 tablespoon **sunflower seeds** and 1 tablespoon **pumpkin seeds** in a dry frying pan over a medium heat for 2-3 minutes until fragrant. Remove from the heat and set aside to cool. In a large bowl, combine 20ml **apple cider vinegar**, 2 tablespoons **olive oil**, 1 tablespoon **lemon juice** and 2 teaspoons **Dijon mustard**. Core and slice 1 **Braeburn apple** into matchsticks, then add to the bowl along with 60g **baby kale**, 160g shredded **Savoy cabbage**, 1 coarsely grated **carrot**, 10g chopped **fresh flat-leaf parsley** and ¼ **red onion**, thinly sliced. Add the toasted seeds to the bowl, season to taste and toss everything together until evenly coated in the dressing.

Spiced courgette soup

serves 4 prep time 10 minutes cook time 30 minutes

  per serving

Glossy green courgettes are cheap, plentiful and versatile – and they keep well, too. In this fuss-free soup, we've sautéed them with ginger and curry powder for a warming twist.

Calorie controlled cooking spray

2 courgettes, trimmed and roughly chopped

4 spring onions, trimmed and finely sliced

3 garlic cloves, finely sliced

2cm piece fresh ginger, finely grated

½ tablespoon mild curry powder

800ml vegetable stock, made with 2 stock cubes

50g young leaf spinach

20g fresh coriander, leaves picked and roughly chopped

Grated zest and juice of 1 lemon

1 teaspoon cumin seeds

45g 0% fat natural Greek yogurt

1 Mist a large pan with cooking spray and fry the courgettes, spring onions and garlic over a medium heat for 5 minutes, until just starting to soften. Add the ginger and curry powder and cook for 2 minutes, then pour in the stock. Bring to the boil then reduce the heat and simmer for 15-20 minutes until the vegetables are tender.

2 Add the spinach and half the coriander to the pan, and cook for 2 minutes until the spinach is wilted. Stir in the lemon zest and juice, then season to taste and remove from the heat. Using a stick blender, blitz the soup until smooth.

3 Meanwhile, toast the cumin seeds in a dry frying pan over a medium heat for 1-2 minutes, until fragrant, then crush slightly using a pestle and mortar.

4 Ladle the soup into bowls, swirl in the yogurt and serve garnished with the toasted cumin seeds and remaining coriander.

Cook's tip
Serve each portion with a 50g mini naan bread. The recipe will no longer be gluten free.

Roasted Tenderstem broccoli salad with cashew dressing

serves 4   prep time 20 minutes + soaking   cook time 45 minutes

  per serving

When it comes to fresh green veg, broccoli is hard to beat. Try it roasted with butternut squash and red onions, served with a creamy cashew dressing.

1 small butternut squash, halved, deseeded and diced

2 red onions, cut into wedges

Calorie controlled cooking spray

1 tablespoon ground coriander

1 teaspoon chilli flakes

200g Tenderstem broccoli

FOR THE CASHEW DRESSING

50g unsalted cashews

1 small garlic clove, crushed

1 green chilli, deseeded and chopped

1 red chilli, deseeded and chopped

1 shallot, chopped

1 tablespoon walnut oil

Grated zest and juice of 1 lemon

25g fresh coriander, chopped

25g fresh basil, chopped

1 To make the cashew dressing, put the cashews in a small bowl, cover with cold water and set aside to soak for 30 minutes. Drain the cashews and put them into a mini food processor or blender with the remaining dressing ingredients. Blitz until smooth and combined, adding a splash of water if the dressing is too thick. Season to taste.

2 Meanwhile, preheat the oven to 220°C, fan 200°C, gas mark 7. Put the butternut squash and onions on a large baking tray, mist all over with cooking spray and scatter over the ground coriander and chilli flakes. Season well, toss everything together and roast for 30 minutes until tender. Add the broccoli to the tray, mist with more cooking spray and roast for another 15 minutes until the broccoli is starting to char. Remove from the oven and let cool slightly, then cut the broccoli into bite-size pieces.

3 To serve, transfer the warm roasted vegetables to a large platter and spoon over the cashew dressing.

Cook's tip

To bulk this up, cook 240g dry quinoa to pack instructions, then toss the grains through the salad.

Spiced squash & cauliflower fritters with red pepper salsa

serves 4 **prep time 15 minutes + chilling** **cook time 25 minutes**

   per serving

Looking for new ways with butternut squash? These flavour-packed flourless fritters, served with a fresh oil-free salsa, make for an impressive meal any time of the day.

400g prepared butternut squash, cut into small pieces

200g small cauliflower florets

4 sprigs fresh thyme, leaves stripped

2 tablespoons chopped fresh flat-leaf parsley

1 tablespoon ground coriander

Calorie controlled cooking spray

Rocket leaves, to serve

FOR THE RED PEPPER SALSA

1 red pepper, deseeded and finely chopped

2 tomatoes, finely chopped

2 spring onions, trimmed and finely sliced

1 tablespoon chopped fresh coriander

Grated zest and juice of 1 lime

1 Put the butternut squash and cauliflower into a large steamer set over a large pan of simmering water. Steam for 10-12 minutes, until the vegetables are tender, then transfer to a large bowl.

2 Using a potato masher, mash the squash and cauliflower together until smooth. Add the thyme, parsley and coriander, then season and mix well. Shape the mixture into 12 patties and chill in the fridge for at least 30 minutes to firm up.

3 Meanwhile, make the red pepper salsa. In a small bowl, combine all the salsa ingredients, then season to taste and set aside.

4 Put a large nonstick frying pan over a medium heat and mist with cooking spray. Fry the fritters in batches, turning carefully and regularly, for 3-4 minutes until golden and starting to crisp.

5 Serve 3 fritters per person with the rocket and red pepper salsa on the side.

Cook's tip
These fritters, served with 1 gently poached egg per serving, make a great brunch option. The recipe will no longer be vegan.

Red cabbage slaw

serves 4   prep time 10 minutes + standing   cook time 5 minutes

  per serving

If you're used to serving slaw on the side, try this zero hero-packed version as a generous main-course salad. It's vibrant, and full of crunch thanks to a sprinkling of toasted seeds.

½ red cabbage, thinly sliced

4 tomatoes, diced

1 cucumber, trimmed and diced

2 carrots, coarsely grated

4 teaspoons sunflower seeds

FOR THE DRESSING

200g 0% fat natural Greek yogurt

Grated zest and juice of ½ lemon

1 tablespoon chopped fresh chives

Cook's tip

This coleslaw will keep in an airtight container in the fridge for up to 2 days.

1   Put the red cabbage in a large bowl, add a large pinch of salt then toss to combine. Using your hands, vigorously massage the cabbage until it begins to soften and release some liquid, then set the bowl aside for 10 minutes.

2   Drain the cabbage, squeeze out any excess liquid and pat dry with kitchen paper. Return the cabbage to the bowl, add the tomatoes, cucumber and carrots, then toss to combine.

3   Meanwhile, toast the sunflower seeds in a dry frying pan over a medium heat for 2-3 minutes, until fragrant, then set aside. To make the dressing, combine all the dressing ingredients in a small bowl, then season to taste.

4   Drizzle the dressing over the coleslaw mixture and serve with the sunflower seeds scattered over.

Roast beetroot burgers

makes 4   **prep time 20 minutes + chilling**   **cook time 55 minutes**

   per burger

If you've never roasted whole beetroot before, you'll be amazed at the extra flavour it brings to a dish. A little goes a long way, as these burgers show.

3 portabella mushrooms, cut into thin strips

Calorie controlled cooking spray

140g whole beetroot, scrubbed

60g frozen green peas, thawed

100g drained and rinsed tinned green or brown lentils

85g cooked brown rice

25g fresh flat-leaf parsley, leaves picked

35g fresh wholemeal breadcrumbs

1 large egg, lightly beaten

3 garlic cloves, finely chopped

2 tablespoons Dijon mustard

2 tablespoons reduced-fat mayonnaise

4 x 60g burger buns, split

30g mixed salad leaves

1 small red onion, sliced

12 dill pickle slices

1   Preheat the oven to 200°C, fan 180°C, gas mark 6. Put the mushrooms on one side of a baking tray and mist with cooking spray. Wrap the beetroot in kitchen foil and put it on the other side of the tray. Bake for 45 minutes or until the mushrooms are dried and the beetroot is tender. Leave the beetroot to cool, then rub off the skin and roughly chop the flesh.

2   Put the beetroot and mushrooms into a food processor with the peas, lentils, rice, parsley, breadcrumbs, egg and garlic. Season, then pulse briefly until the mixture holds together – it should still be chunky, so take care not to over-process. Shape the mixture into 4 patties and chill them in the fridge for 1 hour to firm up.

3   Mist a large nonstick frying pan with cooking spray and cook the beetroot patties over a medium heat for 5 minutes on each side, or until browned.

4   Mix together the mustard and mayonnaise, then spread half of the mixture over the base of each burger bun. Top with the salad leaves followed by the beetroot patties, remaining mustard mayo, onion and pickles. Sandwich with the remaining bun halves and serve.

Cook's tip
To reduce the SmartPoints of this dish, use 1 bun between 2 people and serve as open burgers instead.

Cauliflower 'risotto'

serves 4   prep time 15 minutes   cook time 35 minutes

  per serving

We've discovered another clever way to use the humble cauliflower. Our take on risotto uses cauliflower rice instead of Arborio and a cauliflower purée to add creaminess.

Calorie controlled cooking spray

1 cauliflower, florets roughly chopped (you'll need 650g)

2 garlic cloves, finely chopped

200ml vegetable stock, made with 1 stock cube

12g nutritional yeast

1 large onion, finely chopped

4 sprigs fresh thyme, leaves stripped

250g chestnut mushrooms, sliced

1 tablespoon chopped fresh flat-leaf parsley, to serve

1   Mist a nonstick pan with cooking spray and set over a medium heat. Add one-third of the cauliflower and all the garlic and cook, stirring, for 2-3 minutes. Add the stock, bring the mixture to a simmer and cook, covered, for 15 minutes until the cauliflower is very tender. Remove from the heat, sprinkle over the nutritional yeast, and use a stick blender to blitz the mixture to a smooth purée.

2   Meanwhile, put the remaining cauliflower into a food processor and blitz until roughly the texture of rice, then set aside.

3   Mist a large nonstick frying pan with cooking spray and add the onion, thyme, mushrooms and 2 tablespoons water. Cook, stirring occasionally, for 10 minutes until the vegetables are tender. Add the cauliflower rice and 50ml boiling water from the kettle and cook, stirring, for 2 minutes until hot.

4   Stir the cauliflower purée into the mixture, adding a splash of water if the 'risotto' is too thick.

5   Season to taste and serve garnished with the parsley.

Cook's tip

For a glossier, risotto-like texture, stir ½ teaspoon xanthan gum into the cauliflower mixture in Step 1. You'll need to add it at the same time as the nutritional yeast. The SmartPoints will remain the same.

Griddled lettuce with red pepper pesto & chimichurri

serves 4   prep time 20 minutes   cook time 10 minutes

  per serving

Griddling lettuce might seem like an unusual thing to do, but just a few minutes spent on a hot griddle brings out a whole other flavour dimension. Try it as a side with grilled fish fillets.

Calorie controlled cooking spray

2 Romaine lettuces, halved lengthways

1 lemon, cut into wedges, to serve

FOR THE RED PEPPER PESTO

2 roasted red peppers in brine, drained and roughly chopped (you'll need 200g)

10g fresh flat-leaf parsley, chopped

1 garlic clove, crushed

FOR THE CHIMICHURRI

1 shallot, finely chopped

1 garlic clove, finely chopped

1 green chilli, deseeded and finely diced

1 red chilli, deseeded and finely diced

50ml red wine vinegar

25g fresh coriander, finely chopped

10g fresh flat-leaf parsley, finely chopped

1 tablespoon extra-virgin olive oil

1 To make the red pepper pesto, put all the pesto ingredients into a food processor and blend until smooth. Season to taste and set aside.

2 For the chimichurri, put all the chimichurri ingredients into a small bowl with 2 tablespoons water. Mix until well combined then season to taste and set aside.

3 Heat a large nonstick griddle over a high heat until it starts to smoke. Mist the lettuce with cooking spray then griddle, in batches, for 1-2 minutes on each side, until charred.

4 Put the griddled lettuce on a serving platter, spoon over the red pepper pesto and chimichurri, and serve with the lemon wedges on the side.

Cook's tip

Toast 1 tablespoon each of sunflower and pumpkin seeds in a dry frying pan over a medium heat for 2-3 minutes, until fragrant. Scatter over the lettuce before serving.

Satay vegetable noodles

serves 4   prep time 30 minutes

  2 per serving

Fresh, spicy and full of crunch, this no-cook dish is a great way to make raw zero hero vegetables shine. It's great as a light lunch or served as part of a main course dinner.

½ small red cabbage, shredded

1 large courgette, spiralised

1 carrot, spiralised

1 parsnip, spiralised

2 spring onions, trimmed
and finely sliced

FOR THE SATAY DRESSING

3 tablespoons PBFit Peanut
Butter Powder

Juice of 1 lime

1 tablespoon agave syrup

3 tablespoons tamari sauce

1 teaspoon sesame oil

2 tablespoons rice wine vinegar

1 tablespoon grated ginger

1 tablespoon chilli sauce

Pinch chilli flakes

1 To make the satay dressing, put all the dressing ingredients in a bowl, then stir together with a fork until creamy and combined. Set aside.

2 In a serving bowl, toss together the cabbage, spiralised vegetables and spring onions. Add the satay dressing, toss until evenly coated, then serve.

Cook's tip
For extra protein, top
each portion of noodles
with 50g griddled tofu.

Fruit salad with lime dressing

serves 4   prep time 10 minutes   cook time 5 minutes

  per serving

This fresh salad, packed with ripe, juicy soft fruits, dressed with a simple lime dressing and finished with toasted nuts and fresh mint, is as pleasing to look at as it is to eat.

16 unsalted cashews

300g strawberries, hulled and quartered

250g blueberries

400g pitted cherries, halved

Grated zest and juice of 2 limes

4 teaspoons agave syrup

Handful of chopped fresh mint

1   Toast the cashews in a dry frying pan over a medium heat for 2-3 minutes, until fragrant and golden. Remove from the heat and roughly chop.

2   Put the strawberries, blueberries and cherries into a serving bowl. In a separate small bowl, mix together the lime zest and juice and agave syrup, then add to the fruit and toss to coat.

3   Divide the dressed fruit salad between bowls, scatter over the toasted cashews and mint, then serve.

Plum & pistachio crumble

serves 8   prep time 15 minutes + cooling   cook time 35 minutes

  4 per serving

Nothing is as inviting as the aroma of a fruit-filled crumble wafting from the kitchen. This crumble makes the most of ripe, plump plums and juicy blackberries.

Calorie controlled cooking spray

4 large plums, halved, stones removed and thinly sliced

600g blackberries

1½ tablespoons plain flour

1 teaspoon finely grated lemon zest

¼ teaspoon ground cardamom

100g porridge oats

55g light brown soft sugar

50g dairy-free spread

35g pistachio kernels, finely chopped

1 Preheat the oven to 180°C, fan 160°C, gas mark 4. Mist a medium baking dish with cooking spray.

2 Put the plums, blackberries, flour, lemon zest and cardamom in a large mixing bowl and toss gently to evenly coat the fruit. Spoon the mixture into the prepared baking dish.

3 Combine the oats, sugar, dairy-free spread and a pinch of salt in a medium bowl. Using your fingertips, rub everything together until the mixture clumps, then stir in the pistachios.

4 Scatter the crumble mixture evenly over the fruit, then bake for 30-35 minutes, until the crumble is golden and the fruit filling is bubbling. Set aside to cool for 15 minutes before serving.

Cook's tip
Serve each portion topped with 50g plain soya yogurt. The SmartPoints will remain the same.

Pineapple waffles

serves 4   prep time 5 minutes   cook time 5 minutes

  per serving

Sweet, crunchy and the colour of sunshine, fresh tropical pineapple is guaranteed to raise a smile. Here, it's caramelised to bring out even more sweetness, then spooned over waffles.

1 tablespoon desiccated coconut

2 teaspoons low-fat spread

700g fresh pineapple, finely diced

1 tablespoon maple syrup

1 tablespoon lime juice

4 toasting waffles (we used McVitie's)

4 tablespoons 0% fat natural Greek yogurt

1   Toast the coconut in a small dry frying pan over a medium heat for 1-2 minutes, until fragrant and golden. Remove from the heat and set aside.

2   Melt the low-fat spread in a large nonstick frying pan over a medium-high heat. Cook the pineapple, stirring occasionally, for 3-4 minutes or until most of the liquid evaporates, then add the maple syrup. Cook, stirring, for another 2 minutes until the pineapple is lightly golden, then stir in the lime juice and remove from the heat.

3   Toast the waffles to pack instructions, then divide between plates and serve topped with the caramelised pineapple, yogurt and toasted coconut.

Cook's tip
If you enjoy tropical fruit flavours, spoon over some passion fruit pulp, too. The SmartPoints will remain the same.

Four variations... **Roasted veg**

Let your oven do all the hard work with these easy roasted vegetable recipes – there's a hearty warm salad, colourful dip, earthy soup and a new chip to fall in love with.

Spice-roasted vegetables

serves 4   prep time 15 minutes   cook time 35 minutes

   per serving

Preheat the oven to 220°C, fan 200°C, gas mark 7. Deseed and chop 1 small **butternut squash** into 2cm pieces and put on a large baking tray with 1 chopped **courgette** and 1 deseeded and chopped **red pepper**. Add 2 crushed **garlic** cloves, 1 tablespoon **ground coriander** and 1 teaspoon **ground cumin**. Mist all over with **calorie controlled cooking spray**, then season well and toss to combine. Roast for 35 minutes, or until the squash is tender and the rest of the vegetables are lightly caramelised. Transfer to a serving bowl and toss through 10g each of chopped **fresh flat-leaf parsley**, **coriander** and **mint** leaves. Squeeze over the juice of ½ **lemon**, then season to taste and serve.

Roasted beetroot houmous

serves 8   prep time 10 minutes   cook time 45 minutes

   per serving

Preheat the oven to 200°C, fan 180°C, gas mark 6. Trim and scrub 2 small whole **beetroot** (you'll need about 250g), then wrap each individually in kitchen foil. Roast for 45 minutes, or until tender. Remove from the foil, and let cool slightly before peeling and roughly chopping. Transfer the beetroot to a food processor. Drain and rinse a 400g tin **chickpeas**, then add to the food processor with the juice of 1 **lemon**, 2½ tablespoons **tahini**, 2 crushed **garlic** cloves and ½ teaspoon **ground cumin**. Blitz until almost smooth. With the machine running, gradually drizzle in 1 tablespoon **extra-virgin olive oil** and continue to process until the mixture is completely smooth. Season to taste and serve with a selection of zero hero **vegetable crudités**.

Celeriac soup with ricotta toast

serves 4   prep time 10 minutes   cook time 1 hour

   per serving

Put 560g peeled and chopped **celeriac**, 3 halved **shallots**, 2 unpeeled **garlic** cloves, 1 sprig **fresh rosemary** and 2 **bay leaves** in a roasting tin. Mist with **calorie controlled cooking spray**, season and roast for 45-50 minutes until tender and golden. If the veg starts to char, cover with foil, as burnt bits will make the soup bitter. Heat 1 litre **vegetable stock** (made with 1 stock cube) in a pan. Squeeze the garlic out of its skin and add it to the stock, along with the celeriac and shallots (discard the herbs). Bring to the boil and simmer for 10 minutes then remove from the heat and let cool slightly before blending until smooth. Stir through 2 tablespoons **half-fat crème fraîche** and the juice of 1 **lemon** then season. Toast 2 slices of **rye bread**, spread over 2 tablespoons **ricotta**, scatter with **lemon zest** and season. Cut in half and serve with the soup topped with extra rosemary.

Rosemary swede chips

serves 4   prep time 10 minutes   cook time 45 minutes

   per serving

Preheat the oven to 220°C, fan 200°C, gas mark 7. Peel and cut 550g **swede** into 2cm-wide chips, arrange them on a large baking tray and mist all over with **calorie controlled cooking spray**. Season well and roast for 45 minutes, turning every now and then, until tender and lightly caramelised. Scatter over 1 finely chopped **garlic** clove and the chopped leaves of 1 **fresh rosemary** sprig, then season and toss to combine.

Fish & poultry

48 **Tuna & sweetcorn fritters**
    Tuna melt
    Tuna & courgette salad
    Tuna & watercress salad
50 **Crispy chicken cutlets with tarragon butter vegetables**
52 **Smoky pollock with spinach**
54 **Salt & pepper prawns with mango salsa**
56 **Braised chicken & lentils**
58 **Sea bass with black olive, tomato & basil salsa**
60 **Thai yellow prawn curry**
62 **Grilled chicken with mint chimichurri**
64 **Piri-piri roast chicken flatbreads**
66 **Miso-glazed salmon with braised leeks**
68 **Turkey & hoisin sausage rolls**
    Crispy buttermilk turkey
    Frying pan turkey tacos
    Turkey patties with cauliflower & carrot salad

Four variations... **Tinned tuna**

Make the most of this storecupboard staple in these simple, speedy dishes. They're each ready to eat in 25 minutes or less, making them ideal for busy weekday lunches.

Tuna & sweetcorn fritters

serves 4   prep time 10 minutes   cook time 15 minutes

  per serving

Sift 75g **self-raising flour** into a bowl and season well. Make a well in the centre, then add 1 beaten **egg** and 100ml **skimmed milk**, and beat until you have a smooth batter. Drain a 198g tin of **tuna in spring water** and a 160g tin **sweetcorn**, then add these to the batter with 1 teaspoon **chipotle sauce**, 2 tablespoons chopped **fresh coriander** and 4 drained and finely chopped **jalapeño** slices. Mist a nonstick frying pan with **calorie controlled cooking spray** and set over a medium heat. In two batches, fry 4 heaped tablespoons of the fritter mixture for 2-3 minutes each side, until golden. Meanwhile, to make a salad, put 100g shredded **red cabbage** into a bowl and add the juice of 1 **lime**. Toss to combine and set aside for 5 minutes, then stir in 1 deseeded and sliced **red pepper**, 1 grated **carrot**, 2 tablespoons chopped **fresh coriander**, 1 sliced **red onion** and 50g **young leaf spinach**. Season and serve with 2 fritters per person and some **lime wedges**.

Tuna melt

makes 4   prep time 5 minutes   cook time 5 minutes

  per tuna melt

Preheat the grill to high. Drain a 340g tin **tuna in spring water** and put into a bowl with 4 trimmed and finely chopped **spring onions**, 80g **0% fat natural Greek yogurt** and 2 teaspoons **chilli sauce**. Season and stir to combine. Lightly toast 4 slices **WW Malted Danish Bread** then spoon the tuna mixture over the top. Top each piece of toast with a slice of **WW Reduced Fat Mature Cheese**, then put onto a small baking tray and grill for 1-2 minutes, until the cheese melts. Cut in half and serve topped with a handful of **watercress**.

Tuna & courgette salad

serves 4   prep time 15 minutes   cook time 5 minutes

   per serving

Spiralise or grate 4 **courgettes** and set aside. Cook 500g **green beans** in a pan of boiling water for 3 minutes, then drain and refresh under cold running water. Mist a large nonstick frying pan with **calorie controlled cooking spray** and cook the courgettes over a medium heat for 1-2 minutes until softened, then season and set aside. To make a dressing, mix together 2 tablespoons chopped **fresh flat-leaf parsley**, 2 teaspoons chopped **fresh mint**, 2 tablespoons chopped **fresh basil**, 2 teaspoons chopped **capers**, 1 small finely grated **garlic** clove, ½ teaspoon **Dijon mustard**, the juice of 1 **lemon** and 2 tablespoons **0% fat natural Greek yogurt** in a small bowl. Drain a 340g tin of **tuna in spring water** and put into a serving bowl with the courgettes, beans, 300g halved **cherry tomatoes**, and the dressing. Season, toss to coat, then serve.

Tuna & watercress salad

serves 4   prep time 10 minutes   cook time 5 minutes

   per serving

Toast 2 teaspoons **sesame seeds** in a dry frying pan set over a medium heat for 2-3 minutes, until fragrant and golden, then transfer to a bowl and set aside. Blanch 200g **frozen garden peas** in a pan of boiling water for 3-5 minutes, then drain and refresh under cold running water. To make a dressing, mash the flesh of 1 **avocado** in a small bowl, then mix in 4 tablespoons **0% fat natural Greek yogurt**, the juice of 2 **limes**, 2 tablespoons finely chopped **fresh coriander** and 1 small crushed **garlic** clove, then season to taste. Loosen with a little water if it seems too thick. Drain a 340g tin of **tuna in spring water** and put onto a serving platter with the peas, 80g **watercress** and 50g **pea shoots**. Spoon over the avocado dressing and scatter over the toasted sesame seeds to serve.

Crispy chicken cutlets with tarragon butter vegetables

serves 4   prep time 20 minutes   cook time 20 minutes

  per serving

Crisp and crunchy on the outside, and juicy and tender on the inside – these coated chicken fillets, served with steamed veg tossed with tarragon butter, are great for family meals.

4 x 165g skinless chicken breast fillets

30g plain flour

2 eggs, lightly beaten with a pinch of salt

60g fresh wholemeal breadcrumbs

Calorie controlled cooking spray

2 carrots, cut into batons

200g green beans, trimmed

100g young leaf spinach

20g salted butter, softened

2 tablespoons chopped fresh tarragon

½ lemon, cut into wedges

Cook's tip
Serve each portion with 175g boiled and crushed new potatoes on the side.

1 Preheat the oven to 200°C, fan 180°C, gas mark 6. Line a large baking tray with baking paper.

2 Put the chicken between 2 sheets of clingfilm and bash with a rolling pin to a thickness of 1cm.

3 Put the flour, eggs and breadcrumbs into 3 separate shallow bowls. Dust the chicken in the flour, then dip it in the egg and finally the breadcrumbs to coat. Transfer to the prepared baking tray and mist all over with cooking spray. Bake for 15-20 minutes until cooked through and golden.

4 Meanwhile, put the carrots into a large steamer set over a pan of boiling water. Steam for 6-7 minutes, then add the green beans and steam for another 2-3 minutes, until tender. Add the spinach and steam for 2 minutes, until wilted. Transfer the vegetables to a serving bowl and toss with the butter and tarragon. Season to taste and serve with the chicken and lemon wedges.

Smoky pollock with spinach

serves 4   prep time 15 minutes   cook time 30 minutes

 per serving

Pollock – a sustainable alternative to haddock or cod – is a good fish to have in the freezer. Try it cooked from frozen in this smoky, spicy bake.

Zest and juice of 1 lemon

2 teaspoons smoked paprika

4 garlic cloves, 1 crushed and 3 thinly sliced

½ red chilli, deseeded and finely chopped

1 tablespoon finely chopped fresh flat-leaf parsley

4 x 105g frozen pollock fillets

Calorie controlled cooking spray

1 red onion, thinly sliced

80g chorizo, finely chopped

1 red pepper, deseeded and finely chopped

1 large tomato, roughly chopped

200g young leaf spinach

Cook's tip

Drain and rinse a 400g tin cannellini beans and add to the pan with the tomato in step 4.

1 Preheat the oven to 200°C, fan 180°C, gas mark 6. Line a baking tray with baking paper.

2 In a shallow bowl, mix together half the lemon zest and juice, 1 teaspoon of the smoked paprika, the crushed garlic clove, and the chilli and parsley. Season well, then add the fish to the bowl and turn gently to coat.

3 Put the fish on the prepared baking tray and roast for 25-30 minutes until cooked through.

4 Meanwhile, set a pan over a medium heat and mist with cooking spray. Fry the onion, chorizo, red pepper and sliced garlic cloves, then cook for 5 minutes until starting to soften. Add the tomato, remaining smoked paprika and 150ml boiling water from the kettle. Bring to a simmer and cook for 5 minutes.

5 Add the spinach and cook for 5-8 minutes until wilted. Season to taste and stir through the remaining lemon zest and juice.

6 Divide the vegetables between plates, top with the baked fish and serve.

Salt & pepper prawns with mango salsa

serves 4   prep time 15 minutes   cook time 10 minutes

   per serving

A super-tasty warm-weather dish of Chinese-spiced prawns served with a refreshing mango and chilli salsa, crisp lettuce and a squeeze of lime juice.

2 tablespoons cornflour

1 teaspoon chilli flakes

2 teaspoons black peppercorns

1½ teaspoons Chinese five spice

Large pinch sea salt

250g raw peeled king prawns, deveined

1 tablespoon vegetable oil

1 Little Gem lettuce, leaves separated

Lime wedges, to serve

FOR THE MANGO SALSA

1 mango, peeled, stone removed, and finely diced

2 tomatoes, finely diced

½ cucumber, finely diced

1 red chilli, finely diced

2 garlic cloves, finely chopped

Zest and juice of 1 lime

Large handful coriander, leaves picked and chopped

1 To make the salsa, combine all the salsa ingredients in a small bowl, then season with salt to taste and set aside to allow the flavours to meld.

2 Put the cornflour, chilli flakes, peppercorns, Chinese five spice and sea salt into a mini food processor and blitz until the peppercorns are coarsely ground. Transfer to a bowl and toss with the prawns to coat.

3 Heat the oil in a small nonstick frying pan set over a medium heat. Fry the prawns, in batches, for 1-2 minutes on each side, until cooked through.

4 Divide the lettuce leaves between plates, spoon over the mango salsa and top with the spiced prawns. Serve with the lime wedges on the side.

Cook's tip

If you like, turn this into a substantial salad by cooking 240g brown rice (dry weight) to pack instructions, then draining and tossing it with the prawns, lettuce and salsa.

Braised chicken & lentils

serves 4   prep time 20 minutes   cook time 1 hour

  per serving

A comforting, flavour-packed stew made by braising lean chicken fillets with plenty of fragrant herbs, hearty root vegetables and filling lentils.

1 tablespoon chopped fresh thyme leaves

1 tablespoon chopped fresh oregano leaves

1 tablespoon chopped fresh rosemary leaves

1 teaspoon olive oil

4 x 165g skinless chicken breast fillets, halved horizontally

1 large fennel bulb, trimmed, cored and finely chopped (fronds reserved)

1 onion, finely chopped

1 carrot, finely chopped

1 garlic clove, crushed

100g dried green lentils, rinsed and drained

400ml chicken stock, made with ½ stock cube

4 stalks Swiss chard, leaves stripped and shredded (see Cook's tip)

1 Combine the thyme, oregano and rosemary in a small bowl. Season well.

2 Heat the oil in a deep, nonstick frying pan over a medium-high heat. In batches, brown the chicken for 2 minutes on each side, then transfer to a plate and scatter over the herb mixture.

3 Add the fennel, onion, carrot and garlic to the pan and cook, stirring, for 3 minutes or until the vegetables are golden. Add the lentils and stock and bring to the boil. Return the chicken to the pan, reduce the heat to medium-low and cook, covered, for 35-40 minutes, until the lentils are tender and the chicken is cooked through.

4 Add the Swiss chard and cook, uncovered, for 2 minutes or until wilted. Serve garnished with the reserved fennel fronds.

Cook's tip

To reduce waste, finely slice the Swiss chard stalks and add them to the pan with the lentils in Step 3.

Sea bass with black olive, tomato & basil salsa

serves 4   prep time 15 minutes   cook time 20 minutes

   per serving

We've called on some popular Mediterranean ingredients to create a glorious plate of grilled fish fillets and roasted courgettes, served with a colourful salsa.

2 courgettes, diced

Calorie controlled cooking spray

4 x 120g sea bass fillets

100g young leaf spinach

FOR THE BLACK OLIVE, TOMATO & BASIL SALSA

200g baby plum tomatoes, roughly chopped

80g drained and pitted Kalamata olives in brine, sliced

½ garlic clove, finely chopped

½ red onion, finely diced

1 tablespoon red wine vinegar

1 red chilli, deseeded and finely chopped

Handful fresh basil leaves, roughly torn

1   To make the black olive salsa, combine all the salsa ingredients in a small bowl, then season to taste and set aside.

2   Preheat the oven to 200°C, fan 180°C, gas mark 6. Put the courgettes on a baking tray, mist all over with cooking spray then season and roast for 15-20 minutes, until tender and golden.

3   Heat the grill to high and mist a nonstick baking tray with cooking spray. Put the fish, skin-side up, on the tray then mist with cooking spray and season well. Grill for 4-6 minutes, then gently turn and grill for a final 1 minute.

4   Serve the sea bass with the salsa spooned over the top and the roasted courgettes and spinach on the side.

Cook's tip

Serve with the rosemary swede fries (see recipe, page 44). The SmartPoints will remain the same.

Thai yellow prawn curry

serves 4   prep time 10 minutes   cook time 30 minutes

  per serving

Try this quick-and-easy fragrant curry, made with just eight ingredients, on a busy weeknight when you're short on time.

1 teaspoon vegetable oil

1 tablespoon Thai yellow curry paste

400g tin chopped tomatoes

450g prepared butternut squash, cut into 2cm pieces

400g green beans, trimmed

350g raw king prawns, peeled with tails left on

400g cauliflower florets

Handful coriander, leaves picked and chopped

Cook's tip

Instead of cauliflower rice, serve this curry with 240g brown rice (dry weight), cooked to pack instructions.

1   Heat the oil in a nonstick wok or frying pan over a medium-high heat. Add the curry paste and cook, stirring, for 30 seconds or until fragrant. Stir in the tomatoes and 250ml water, then add the butternut squash and bring to the boil.

2   Reduce the heat and simmer, uncovered, for 15-20 minutes or until the butternut squash is tender – if the curry sauce gets too thick, you may need to add a splash of water.

3   Add the beans and prawns to the wok, then cover and simmer for 3 minutes or until the beans are just tender and the prawns are cooked through.

4   Meanwhile, blitz the cauliflower in a food processor until it's roughly the texture of rice. Transfer to a large microwave-safe bowl, cover and microwave on High for 5 minutes, or until tender.

5   Divide the cauliflower rice between bowls, top with the curry and serve garnished with the coriander.

Grilled chicken with mint chimichurri

serves 4   **prep time 10 minutes**   **cook time 20 minutes**

  per serving

A simple grilled chicken breast supper livened up with a spoonful or two of chimichurri – a spicy green sauce made with fresh herbs, garlic, vinegar, chillies and olive oil.

Calorie controlled cooking spray

4 x 165g skinless chicken breast fillets

½ teaspoon ground cumin

FOR THE MINT CHIMICHURRI

20g fresh mint leaves, chopped

10g fresh flat-leaf parsley, chopped

3 tablespoons white wine vinegar

1 tablespoon olive oil

2 garlic cloves, finely chopped

¾ teaspoon chilli flakes

1 To make the chimichurri, put all the chimichurri ingredients into a food processor with 1 tablespoon water and blitz until combined. Season to taste then set aside.

2 Heat the grill to high. Mist the chicken with cooking spray, scatter over the cumin and season well. Transfer the chicken to a large, nonstick ovenproof griddle pan and cook under the grill for 15-20 minutes, turning once, until the chicken is cooked through.

3 Serve the chicken topped with the chimichurri.

Cook's tip

Serve with lettuce and a fresh tomato and red onion salsa on the side. The SmartPoints will remain the same.

Piri-piri roast chicken flatbreads

serves 4   prep time 10 minutes + resting   cook time 30 minutes

   per serving

Enjoy all the flavours of piri-piri chicken flatbreads at home, with our oven-baked version of the popular takeaway dish.

2 tablespoons piri-piri seasoning

Grated zest and juice of 1 lemon

3 garlic cloves, crushed

4 x 165g skinless chicken breast fillets

3 tablespoons 0% fat natural Greek yogurt

½ teaspoon smoked paprika

2 Romaine lettuces, finely sliced

4 tomatoes, finely diced

½ cucumber, finely diced

1 red onion, thinly sliced

4 x 35g wholemeal folded flatbreads (we used Sainsbury's)

1 Preheat the oven to 200°C, fan 180°C, gas mark 6.

2 In a bowl, mix together the piri-piri seasoning, half the lemon zest, half the lemon juice and two-thirds of the garlic, then season well. Put the chicken on a baking tray, spread over the piri-piri mixture then bake for 25-30 minutes, until cooked through and golden. Let rest for at least 5 minutes before thickly slicing.

3 Combine the yogurt and paprika with the remaining lemon zest and garlic, then season to taste.

4 In a bowl, toss together the lettuce, tomatoes, cucumber, red onion and remaining lemon juice.

5 Toast the flatbreads and fill with the chicken, salad and yogurt dressing.

Cook's tip

Reduce the SmartPoints by serving the chicken, salad and yogurt dressing without the flatbreads.

Miso-glazed salmon with braised leeks

serves 4   prep time 15 minutes   cook time 15 minutes

  per serving

An ideal dish to make for guests, these baked salmon fillets with a sweet-and-savoury miso glaze are served with butter-braised leeks on the side.

4 x 130g salmon fillets

2 teaspoons grated ginger

1½ teaspoons light soy sauce

1 tablespoon butter, softened

1½ tablespoons white miso paste

1 teaspoon clear honey

1 teaspoon rice vinegar

2 spring onions, trimmed and sliced

Handful coriander leaves, to serve

FOR THE BRAISED LEEKS

3 large leeks, trimmed and thinly sliced

2 teaspoons butter, softened

1 Preheat the oven to 200°C, fan 180°C, gas mark 6.

2 To make the braised leeks, combine the leeks, butter and 25ml water in a large nonstick pan, then season well. Cook, stirring regularly, over a medium heat for 10 minutes, until soft and translucent.

3 Meanwhile, put the salmon on a baking tray. Combine 1 teaspoon of the ginger with the soy sauce and spoon over the salmon. Bake for 10-12 minutes, until the salmon is cooked through.

4 While the leeks are braising and the salmon is baking, combine the butter, remaining ginger, miso paste, honey and rice vinegar in a small bowl. Spoon the butter over the salmon and return to the oven to bake for a final 2 minutes.

5 Divide the leeks between plates, top with the salmon and serve garnished with the spring onions and coriander.

Cook's tip

For a more substantial dish, fold the braised leeks through 400g boiled and mashed potatoes (no added ingredients).

Four variations... **Turkey breast**

Whether minced or portioned into lean steaks, skinless turkey breast fillet can be used in all kinds of different ways, as these four clever recipes show.

Turkey & hoisin sausage rolls

makes 24   **prep time 10 minutes**   **cook time 25 minutes**

  per sausage roll

Preheat the oven to 200°C, fan 180°C, gas mark 6. Line 2 baking trays with baking paper. Unroll 375g **ready rolled light puff pastry** and cut in half lengthways to give you 2 long pieces. Brush each piece with 1 tablespoon **hoisin sauce**, leaving a 1cm border around the edges. In a bowl, combine 500g **turkey breast mince** with 2 chopped **garlic** cloves and 4 chopped **spring onions**, then season well. Shape the filling into 2 logs that will run the length of the pastry sheets, then place them down the middle of each. Beat 1 **egg** and use a little of it to brush the far edges of the pastry, then fold the pastry over the filling and seal. Roll until the join is underneath, then cut each log into 12 pieces. Arrange on the prepared baking trays, brush the tops with the remaining egg and scatter over 1 teaspoon **mixed black and white sesame seeds**. Bake for 25 minutes, or until crisp and golden.

Crispy buttermilk turkey

serves 4   **prep time 20 minutes**   **cook time 25 minutes**

  per serving

Preheat the oven to 200°C, fan 180°C, gas mark 6. Line a baking tray with baking paper. In a bowl, whisk together 60ml **buttermilk**, 1 teaspoon **smoked paprika**, 1 crushed **garlic** clove and ½ teaspoon **dried thyme**, then season well. Put 50g **plain flour** onto a plate. Working in batches, dip 4 x 125g **skinless turkey breast fillet** portions into the buttermilk mixture, followed by the flour, then put onto the prepared baking tray. Mist with **calorie controlled cooking spray** and bake for 20-25 minutes until cooked through and golden. Meanwhile, to make a slaw, mix together ½ shredded small **red cabbage**, 2 grated **carrots**, 3 shredded **spring onions**, 1 deseeded and sliced **red pepper** and 1 tablespoon **white wine vinegar**. Season to taste and serve with the buttermilk turkey and some **lemon** wedges.

Frying pan turkey tacos

serves 4   **prep time 5 minutes**   **cook time 20 minutes**

   per serving

Mist a large nonstick frying pan with **calorie controlled cooking spray** and fry 500g **turkey breast mince** over a medium-high heat for 5 minutes, until browned. Add 1 diced **onion** and 1 deseeded and diced **red pepper** and cook, stirring, for 5 minutes. Stir in 30g **taco seasoning mix**, then add a 400g tin **chopped tomatoes** and cook for 3 minutes – add a splash of water if the mixture is dry. Stir in 100g **young leaf spinach** and 2 **WW Wholemeal Wraps**, cut into bite-size squares using kitchen scissors, and cook for 2 minutes, or until the spinach is wilted. Season to taste and scatter over 80g **WW Reduced Fat Grated Mature Cheese**. Cook for 2-3 minutes, until the cheese is almost melted, then scatter over 2 tablespoons chopped **fresh coriander**, 2 chopped **spring onions** and 2 tablespoons sliced **jalapeño**. Serve with **lime** wedges on the side.

Turkey patties with cauliflower & carrot salad

serves 4   **prep time 15 minutes**   **cook time 20 minutes**

  per serving

In a bowl, mix together 500g **turkey breast mince**, 1 finely chopped **onion** and 2 teaspoons **ras el hanout**. Season then stir in 2 tablespoons chopped **fresh flat-leaf parsley**. Shape the mince into 12 balls, then flatten slightly. Mist a large nonstick frying pan with **calorie controlled cooking spray** and cook the patties for 5-10 minutes, turning until browned all over. Add 2 teaspoons **harissa paste** followed by a 400g tin **chopped tomatoes**. Stir and cook over a low heat, covered, for 10 minutes. Coarsely grate 400g **cauliflower florets** and 1 **carrot**, then toss in a bowl with 1 tablespoon chopped **fresh flat-leaf parsley** and 1 teaspoon **ground cumin**. Season and divide between plates, then top with the turkey patties and serve garnished with some extra parsley.

Pulses & grains

72 Blueberry & coconut flapjacks

74 Bulgur wheat tabbouleh with courgette & houmous

76 Butter bean fritters with yogurt & cucumber dip

78 Mushroom, spinach & lentil lasagne

80 Quinoa with sticky harissa aubergine & pomegranate

82 Chickpea peanut butter cookies

84 Butternut squash & kale curry

86 Red lentil crisps

Puy lentil bowl

Puy lentil & edamame salad

Green lentil & spinach polpette

Blueberry & coconut flapjacks

makes 10   prep time 5 minutes   cook time 50 minutes

  per flapjack

Porridge oats can be used for so much more than filling your breakfast bowl. They're especially tasty when toasted and baked – try them in these deliciously chewy fruit flapjacks.

55g low-fat spread

50g light muscovado sugar

1 very ripe banana, mashed (you'll need 100g)

175g porridge oats

25g desiccated coconut

40g blueberries

1 Preheat the oven to 170°C, fan 150°C, gas mark 3. Grease and line a 10cm x 20cm baking tin with baking paper.

2 Put the low-fat spread and sugar into a small pan and warm over a medium heat until melted and combined. Add the banana and stir until combined.

3 Remove from the heat and stir in the oats and coconut until well combined. Spoon the mixture into the prepared tin and press it evenly into the corners of the tin using the back of the spoon. Scatter the blueberries over the top and gently press into the flapjack mixture. Bake for 45 minutes, until just turning golden at the edges.

4 Remove from the oven, and let cool in the tin before cutting into 10 flapjacks.

The flapjacks will keep in an airtight container for up to 5 days, or frozen for up to 3 months.

Bulgur wheat tabbouleh with courgette & houmous

serves 4   prep time 10 minutes + standing   cook time 15 minutes

  per serving

The nutty flavour and firm texture of bulgur wheat are well suited to salads. Here, we've boosted a classic tabbouleh with zero heroes courgette and pomegranate.

60g bulgur wheat, rinsed well

Large bunch fresh flat-leaf parsley (you'll need 100g)

Bunch fresh mint (you'll need 30g)

200g tomatoes, finely chopped

6 spring onions, trimmed and chopped

Juice of 2 lemons

1 tablespoon olive oil

Calorie controlled cooking spray

2 courgettes, halved and peeled into ribbons using a vegetable peeler

80g reduced-fat houmous, to serve

4 tablespoons pomegranate seeds, to serve

1 Bring a small pan of water to the boil, add the bulgur wheat and cook for 7-8 minutes until just tender – it should still have some bite. Drain and refresh under cold running water, then drain again. Press any excess moisture out using the back of a spoon.

2 Transfer the bulgur wheat to a large bowl and mix in the herbs, tomatoes, spring onions, lemon juice, oil and a large pinch of salt. Season with freshly ground black pepper and set aside for 10 minutes to allow the bulgur to soak up the dressing.

3 Meanwhile, heat a large nonstick griddle pan over a high heat. Mist the courgette ribbons with cooking spray and griddle for 1-2 minutes until tender and charred – you'll need to do this in batches.

4 To serve, spread the houmous over a large serving plate, spoon over the tabbouleh, top with the courgette and scatter over the pomegranate seeds.

Cook's tip

If you like, crumble over 80g light feta before serving. The dish will no longer be vegan or dairy free.

Butter bean fritters with yogurt & cucumber dip

serves 4 **prep time 15 minutes** **cook time 15 minutes**

  per serving

Turn a tin of creamy butter beans into a batch of tasty fritters with little more than a few storecupboard flavour boosters, then serve with an easy cucumber and yogurt dip on the side.

400g tin butter beans, drained and rinsed

4 spring onions, trimmed and chopped

1 garlic clove, roughly chopped

2 tablespoons finely chopped fresh flat-leaf parsley

1 tablespoon chargrilled red pepper paste (we used Sainsbury's)

1 teaspoon ground cumin

1 teaspoon paprika

Grated zest of ½ lemon

Mixed salad leaves, to serve

FOR THE YOGURT & CUCUMBER DIP

150g 0% fat natural Greek yogurt

150g cucumber, diced

1 green chilli, chopped

2 teaspoons chopped fresh mint

Juice of ½ lemon

1 Preheat the oven to 200°C, fan 180°C, gas mark 6. Line a baking tray with baking paper.

2 Put the butter beans, spring onions, garlic, parsley, red pepper paste, cumin, paprika and lemon zest into a food processor. Season, then blitz until smooth and well combined. Shape the mixture into 8 balls, flatten into patties and put onto the prepared baking tray. Bake for 15 minutes, until just turning golden.

3 Meanwhile, to make the dip, mix together the yogurt with two-thirds of the cucumber, chilli and mint in a small bowl. Stir in the lemon juice and season to taste, then top with the remaining cucumber, chilli and mint.

4 Serve 2 butter bean fritters per person with the yogurt dip and some salad leaves on the side.

Cook's tip

If you don't have red pepper paste, you could use red pesto, green pesto, harissa paste or tomato purée instead. Just remember to adjust the SmartPoints.

Mushroom, spinach & lentil lasagne

serves 4   prep time 15 minutes   cook time 1 hour 15 minutes

  per serving

Up your grains, pulses and protein intake with this veggie lasagne that uses pasta sheets made from yellow lentil and brown rice flour instead of regular wheat-based pasta.

Calorie controlled cooking spray

500g mixed mushrooms (such as chestnut and portabella), sliced

2 garlic cloves, chopped

1½ teaspoons dried oregano

½ teaspoon dried thyme

30g plain flour

350ml vegetable stock, made with 1 stock cube

400g young leaf spinach

350g quark

50g WW Reduced Fat Grated Mature Cheese

¼ teaspoon grated nutmeg

6 WW Yellow Lentil Lasagne Sheets

Why not try...
WW Yellow Lentil Lasagne Sheets, made from yellow lentil and brown rice flour, are gluten free and high in protein. Available at the WW online shop.

Cook's tip
To make this recipe gluten free, use gluten-free plain flour in step 2. The SmartPoints will remain the same.

1 Put a large nonstick frying pan over a medium heat and mist with cooking spray. Fry the mushrooms, in batches, for 5-8 minutes, until golden. Return all the mushrooms to the pan, then add the garlic, 1 teaspoon of the oregano and all the thyme, and cook for 1 minute.

2 Stir in the flour and cook for 1 minute, then add the stock, a little at a time, stirring constantly. Bring the mixture to the boil and stir in the spinach leaves – you'll need to add the spinach in batches. Reduce to a simmer and cook for 2 minutes, then season to taste and remove from the heat.

3 Preheat the oven to 190°C, fan 170°C, gas mark 5. Put the quark into a bowl, add 40g of the cheese and all the nutmeg, then season well and stir to combine.

4 To assemble the lasagne, spoon half of the mushroom and spinach mixture into a 1.5 litre baking dish and top with 3 lentil lasagne sheets. Spoon over half of the quark mixture, then repeat with the remaining mushroom mixture and lasagne sheets.

5 Loosen the remaining quark and cheese mixture with 2 tablespoons water, then spread the mixture over the lasagne. Scatter over the remaining cheese and oregano, then bake for 40-45 minutes, until the pasta is tender and the quark topping is golden brown.

Wrap the uncooked lasagne tightly in kitchen foil followed by clingfilm, and freeze for up to 3 months.

Quinoa with sticky harissa aubergine & pomegranate

serves 4   prep time 10 minutes   cook time 45 minutes

   per serving

This sticky, sweet aubergine and watercress salad is a great way to enjoy tricolour quinoa – tiny red, white and black grain-like seeds that have a springy texture and are completely gluten free.

2 aubergines, trimmed and cut into 2cm pieces (you'll need about 650g)

Calorie controlled cooking spray

30g agave syrup

25g harissa paste

2 teaspoons tomato purée

1 tablespoon tamari sauce

120g tricolour quinoa

40g watercress

80g pomegranate seeds

2 tablespoons chopped fresh coriander, plus extra to garnish

3 spring onions, trimmed and thinly sliced

1 Preheat the oven to 200°C, fan 180°C, gas mark 6. Put the aubergine onto a large baking tray and mist with cooking spray. Season and roast for 25-30 minutes.

2 In a small bowl, combine the agave syrup, harissa paste, tomato purée and tamari sauce, then pour the mixture over the aubergine. Continue to cook for 10-15 minutes, stirring halfway, until the aubergine is sticky and golden.

3 Meanwhile, cook the quinoa to pack instructions, then set aside to cool.

4 In a large bowl, toss the quinoa with the watercress, pomegranate seeds, coriander and spring onions. Divide between plates and serve topped with the aubergines and garnished with the extra coriander.

Chickpea peanut butter cookies

makes 16   prep time 10 minutes   cook time 20 minutes

  per cookie

These clever cookies are made using chickpeas and a combination of chocolate and nuts to make them taste incredibly indulgent.

215g tin chickpeas, drained and rinsed

30g smooth peanut butter

1 teaspoon vanilla extract

3 Medjool dates, pitted and finely chopped (you'll need 65g)

1 egg

20g walnuts, finely chopped

25g dark chocolate, chopped

1　Preheat the oven to 180°C, fan 160°C, gas mark 4. Line a baking tray with baking paper.

2　Put the chickpeas, peanut butter, vanilla extract, dates and egg into a food processor with a pinch of salt, and blitz until a thick batter forms. Add half the walnuts and chocolate and pulse 2-3 times until just combined.

3　Drop small tablespoonfuls of the batter onto the baking tray, leaving enough space in between for the cookies to expand when baking. Flatten slightly with the back of the spoon, then top with the remaining walnuts and chocolate, lightly pressing them into the cookie batter.

4　Bake for 15-20 minutes or until golden, then let cool on a wire rack before serving.

The cookies will keep in an airtight container for up to five days.

Butternut squash & kale curry

serves 4   prep time 10 minutes   cook time 45 minutes

  per serving

An incredibly simple one-pot vegan curry that gets its sweetness from butternut squash and coconut, heat from a trio of spices and heartiness from red lentils.

1 teaspoon olive oil

1 onion, chopped

1 leek, trimmed, halved lengthways and thinly sliced

2 teaspoons medium curry powder

1 teaspoon ground cumin

½ teaspoon ground coriander

750ml vegetable stock, made with 1 stock cube

500g prepared butternut squash, diced

150g dried red lentils, rinsed and drained

200g chopped curly kale

125ml reduced-fat coconut milk

1 Heat the oil in a large nonstick pan over a low heat. Add the onion and leek, and cook, covered, for 10 minutes, until softened. Add the curry powder, ground cumin and ground coriander and cook for 1 minute, then add the stock and butternut squash. Bring to the boil, then reduce to a simmer and cook, uncovered, for 10 minutes.

2 Stir in the lentils and continue to cook for 15 minutes, until the lentils are tender. Stir in the kale and coconut milk, and cook for a further 5 minutes, until the kale is tender, then serve.

Cook's tip

Cook 240g brown rice (dry weight) to pack instructions and serve alongside the curry.

Four variations... **Lentils**

Whether they're tinned or dried, red, green or Puy, hearty lentils can be used in all kinds of different ways – from crisps and polpette for snacking to salads and bowls for lunching.

Red lentil crisps

serves 4
prep time 5 minutes + soaking   cook time 45 minutes

 3 **0** **0**   per serving

Soak 125g **dried red lentils** in 200ml cold water for up to 12 hours. Transfer the lentils and their soaking liquid to a food processor and add 1 tablespoon **tomato purée**, 1 teaspoon **smoked paprika**, 3 chopped **spring onions**, 1 halved **garlic** clove and 1 teaspoon **maple syrup**. Blitz until smooth, then add 2 tablespoons chopped **fresh coriander**, season and blitz again until combined. Preheat the oven to 180°C, fan 160°C, gas mark 4. Line a 28cm x 35cm baking tray with baking paper and pour the lentil mixture onto the baking paper. Bake for 30 minutes, then remove from the oven and reduce the temperature to 170°C, fan 150°C, gas mark 3. Use a knife to cut the baked lentils into triangles, then return to the oven and bake for a further 15 minutes, turning halfway, until crisp. Remove from the oven and let cool slightly before serving.

Puy lentil bowl

serves 4   prep time 15 minutes   cook time 45 minutes

 9 **5** **2**   per serving

Preheat the oven to 200°C, fan 180°C, gas mark 6. Cut 400g **sweet potato** into chunks, put on a baking tray and mist with **calorie controlled cooking spray**. Season and roast for 25 minutes, then add 200g **broccoli** florets to the tray, mist with more cooking spray and roast for another 15 minutes, until the broccoli is charred. Scatter over 1 teaspoon **sesame seeds** and roast for a final 5 minutes. Meanwhile, bring a pan of water to the boil. Add 200g **Puy lentils** and cook for 20-25 minutes until tender. Drain and set aside. In a bowl, toss 100g thinly sliced **red cabbage** with the juice of 1 **lemon** then season and set aside to soften a little. To make a dressing, whisk together 4 teaspoons **olive oil** and 1½ teaspoons **lemon juice** then season to taste. To assemble, divide the lentils between bowls, then top with the roasted vegetables, cabbage and 1 **carrot**, peeled into ribbons. Drizzle over the dressing and serve.

Puy lentil & edamame salad

serves 4   prep time 10 minutes   cook time 25 minutes

 8 **1** **1**   per serving

Bring a large pan of water to the boil, add 250g **Puy lentils** and cook for 20-25 minutes, until tender. Drain. In a separate small pan of boiling water, cook 150g **frozen edamame** for 3 minutes, then drain and refresh under cold running water. In a bowl, toss the lentils and edamame with 1 deseeded and sliced **red pepper**, 3 trimmed and sliced **spring onions**, 150g shredded **Chinese cabbage**, 2 tablespoons chopped **fresh basil** and 3 tablespoons chopped **fresh coriander**, then set aside. To make a dressing, combine 2 tablespoons **PBFit Peanut Butter Powder** with 1½ tablespoons water, then put the mixture into a mini food processor with 1 tablespoon **maple syrup**, 1 teaspoon grated **ginger**, ½ teaspoon grated **garlic**, 1 chopped **red chilli** and the juice of 2 **limes**. Blitz until combined, then drizzle over the salad and serve.

Green lentil & spinach polpette

serves 4   prep time 15 minutes   cook time 20 minutes

 4 **1** **1**   per serving

Preheat the oven to 200°C, fan 180°C, gas mark 6. Put 400g **young leaf spinach** into a plastic food bag, seal then pierce the bag. Microwave for 1-2 minutes on High until wilted. Let cool, then squeeze out any liquid and chop. In a bowl, mix the spinach with 1 beaten **egg**, 30g grated **vegetarian Italian hard-style cheese**, 1 chopped **garlic** clove, 50g **quark**, 1 chopped **red chilli** and 2 tablespoons chopped **fresh flat-leaf parsley**. Drain and rinse a 400g tin **green lentils**, then mash and add to the bowl. Season and combine, then roll into 16 walnut-size balls and put on a baking tray. Mist with **calorie controlled cooking spray** and bake for 15 minutes. Meanwhile, make a raita by mixing 350g **0% fat natural Greek yogurt**, ½ diced **cucumber**, the juice of ½ **lemon** and 1 tablespoon chopped **fresh mint**. Serve 4 polpette per person with the raita and **salad** on the side.

Eggs & dairy

90 Herb & feta muffins
92 Coddled eggs
94 Turkish eggs
96 Mushroom miso ramen
98 Frisée salad with bacon & egg
100 Squidgy lemon polenta cake
Chocolate fudge pops
Fro-yo bark
Harissa dip

Herb & feta muffins

Makes 8   prep time 15 minutes   cook time 25 minutes

   per muffin

Packed with fragrant herbs and salty feta, these savoury yogurt muffins can be enjoyed as an on-the-go breakfast, afternoon snack or served on the side of a bowl of soup.

200g self-raising flour

½ teaspoon baking powder

½ teaspoon salt

150g 0% fat natural Greek yogurt

2 tablespoons olive oil

120ml semi-skimmed milk, plus an extra 2 tablespoons

2 eggs

80g light feta, crumbled

3 tablespoons finely chopped fresh flat-leaf parsley

1 teaspoon chopped fresh thyme

YOU WILL ALSO NEED

8 x WW 2 in 1 Mini Cake Moulds

Why not try...

WW 2 in 1 Mini Cake Moulds are reusable silicone baking cases that are perfect for muffins and cupcakes. You can fold the tops over to make mini tart and quiche cases. Available at the WW online shop.

1 Preheat the oven to 180°C, fan 160°C, gas mark 4. Arrange the cake moulds on a baking tray.

2 Sift the flour and baking powder into a large bowl. Add the salt and stir to combine. Make a well in the centre.

3 Put the yogurt, oil and milk into a jug. Add the eggs and beat with a fork to combine.

4 Add the wet mixture to the dry mixture and whisk together until almost combined – don't over-mix. The mixture should drop off the spoon easily – if it seems too thick, add the extra milk to loosen it.

5 Gently stir in three-quarters of the feta, all of the herbs and some freshly ground black pepper. Divide the mixture evenly between the moulds then scatter over the remaining feta. Bake for 22-25 minutes until the muffins are risen and golden.

6 Leave to cool for 5 minutes before gently removing from the moulds to serve.

The muffins will keep for 1-2 days in an airtight container, or they can be frozen for up to 1 month.

Coddled eggs

serves 4   prep time 15 minutes   cook time 15 minutes

   per serving

Creamy, rich and decadent – try coddled eggs and you won't look back. Oven-cooked in ramekins within a *bain marie*, this gentle approach makes ultra-soft eggs that are perfect for dipping.

100g young leaf spinach

Calorie controlled cooking spray

4 large eggs

4 tablespoons Elmlea Single Cream Alternative

Freshly grated nutmeg

1 tablespoon chopped fresh dill

4 slices WW Soft Malted Danish bread

100g smoked salmon

Lemon wedges, to serve

1   Preheat the oven to 180°C, fan 160°C fan, gas mark 4. Rinse the spinach and add to a pan, cover with a lid and cook over a low heat for 1 minute until wilted, stirring once or twice. Leave to cool slightly, then squeeze out any excess liquid and roughly chop.

2   Mist 4 x 175ml ramekins with cooking spray, and divide the spinach between them. Crack an egg into each, then top each egg with 1 tablespoon cream alternative. Season well, then grate over a little nutmeg and scatter over some of the chopped dill.

3   Put the ramekins into a small roasting tin and pour freshly boiled water from the kettle into the roasting tin until it comes halfway up the sides of the ramekins. Cover the tin tightly with a sheet of kitchen foil and carefully transfer the tin to the oven.

4   Bake for 10-12 minutes until the egg whites are set, and the yolks are soft. Ovens vary, so check the eggs after 10 minutes, and if almost set, carefully remove from the water bath and set aside for 1 minute.

5   To serve, toast the bread and top with the smoked salmon. Scatter the remaining dill over the coddled eggs and serve with the smoked salmon toast and lemon wedges on the side

Why not try...

WW Soft Malted Danish – a delicious loaf that's low in SmartPoints and has a distinctive flavour and aroma thanks to a combo of flaked malted wheat ingredients. Available in selected supermarkets.

Turkish eggs

serves 4   prep time 10 minutes   cook time 10 minutes

   per serving

Soft poached eggs with a luscious layer of yogurt, chilli oil and coriander. Served with a toasted wholemeal naan for dipping, these Turkish eggs make for a very special brunch.

300g 0% fat natural Greek yogurt

½ garlic clove, crushed

Finely grated zest of ½ lemon, plus 1 tablespoon juice

4 teaspoons olive oil

1 red chilli, thinly sliced

½ teaspoon smoked paprika, plus extra to serve

1 teaspoon white wine vinegar

4 eggs

2 tablespoons chopped fresh coriander

1 Put the yogurt into a small bowl, stir in the garlic, lemon zest and juice, then season and set aside.

2 Put the oil in a small pan, add most of the fresh chilli and all of the smoked paprika, then warm gently over a low heat until fragrant and just beginning to sizzle. Don't allow the chilli to burn – you just want to infuse the oil with the flavours. Remove from the heat and set aside.

3 Bring a large pan of water to the boil, add the vinegar and reduce the heat to a simmer. Crack the eggs, one at a time, into the simmering water and poach for 3 minutes until the whites are just set and the yolks are still soft. Remove the eggs with a slotted spoon and put on a plate lined with kitchen paper.

4 Divide the yogurt between bowls. Top each with a poached egg, then drizzle 1 teaspoon of the infused oil over each egg. Scatter over the coriander and remaining chilli and serve sprinkled with the extra smoked paprika.

Cook's tip

Serve each portion with a 30g toasted mini wholemeal pitta bread on the side. The recipe will no longer be gluten free.

Mushroom miso ramen

serves 4   prep time 20 minutes   cook time 20 minutes

   per serving

When you're looking for a satisfying supper in a bowl, this warming miso and mixed mushroom broth with wholewheat noodles, tender kale and soft-boiled eggs, hits the spot.

1 teaspoon sesame seeds

Calorie controlled cooking spray

250g chestnut mushrooms, sliced

120g shiitake mushrooms, sliced

1 red chilli, deseeded and finely sliced, plus extra sliced chilli to serve

2 large garlic cloves, sliced

20g piece root ginger, chopped

1.5 litres hot vegetable stock, made with 2 vegetable stock cubes

3 tablespoons white miso paste

4 eggs

4 x 50g nests wholewheat noodles (we used Blue Dragon)

200g kale, stalks removed, and leaves roughly chopped

6 spring onions, trimmed and thinly sliced

1 tablespoon soy sauce

1   Toast the sesame seeds in a dry frying pan for 2-3 minutes, until fragrant and golden. Remove from the heat and set aside.

2   Mist a large nonstick pan with cooking spray and set over a high heat. Add half the mushrooms and cook, for 2-3 minutes, until browned. Transfer to a plate and mist the pan with more cooking spray, then cook the remaining mushrooms. Return all the mushrooms to the pan.

3   Reduce the heat to medium, add the chilli, garlic and ginger, and stir-fry everything for 2 minutes, until fragrant, then add the hot stock. Stir in the miso paste and bring to the boil, then reduce the heat and let the broth simmer while you cook the eggs.

4   Bring a pan of water to the boil, then reduce to a simmer. Add the eggs and cook for 3-4 minutes. Drain the pan then fill again with cold water and set aside for a few minutes to allow the eggs to cool. Drain, then peel and set aside.

5   While the eggs are cooking, add the noodles to the broth, cook for 3 minutes, then add the kale and half the spring onions. Simmer for 2 minutes until the kale and noodles are tender. Stir in the soy sauce.

6   Divide the noodles and veg between bowls and ladle over the broth. Halve the boiled eggs and add to the bowls. Scatter over the remaining spring onions, toasted sesame seeds and extra chilli, then serve.

Frisée salad with bacon & egg

serves 4   prep time 10 minutes   cook time 10 minutes

   per serving

Our low SmartPoints take on a classic French bistro salad uses lean bacon medallions in place of fatty lardons and a low-oil, honey-and-mustard dressing.

Calorie controlled cooking spray

**8 extra-lean smoked
bacon medallions**

1 tablespoon white wine vinegar

4 large eggs

**1 frisée lettuce, trimmed and torn,
or 200g mixed salad leaves**

FOR THE DRESSING

1 tablespoon white wine vinegar

½ tablespoon Dijon mustard

¼ teaspoon honey, optional

**75ml chicken stock, made
with ½ stock cube, cooled**

1 tablespoon olive oil

1 small garlic clove, crushed

1   Mist a large nonstick frying pan with cooking spray and set over a medium heat. Fry the bacon for 3-4 minutes, turning halfway, until crisp. Remove from the heat and set aside.

2   To make the dressing, whisk the white wine vinegar with the mustard, honey (if using), cooled chicken stock, oil and garlic. Season to taste and set aside.

3   Bring a large pan of water to the boil, add the vinegar and reduce the heat to a simmer. Crack the eggs, one at a time, into the simmering water and poach for 3 minutes until the whites are just set and the yolks are still soft. Remove the eggs with a slotted spoon and put on a plate lined with kitchen paper.

4   Put the lettuce or salad leaves into a large bowl and pour over the dressing. Toss to coat, then divide between plates. Scatter over the bacon, top with the poached eggs and season to serve.

Four variations... **Yogurt**

We've folded 0% fat natural Greek yogurt – one of the most versatile ingredients on the ZeroPoint foods list – into frozen desserts, a spicy dip and a moist polenta cake.

Squidgy lemon polenta cake

serves 12   **prep time 15 minutes**   **cook time 50 minutes**

  7 7 7 per serving

Preheat the oven to 180°C, fan 160°C, gas mark 4. Grease and line a 20cm cake tin with baking paper. Put 120g chopped **dried apricots** in a heatproof bowl, pour over 100ml boiling water and set aside for 10 minutes. Tip the apricots and their soaking liquid into a food processor and blitz until smooth. Add 75ml **rapeseed oil**, 60ml **lemon juice**, 3 **eggs** and 150g **0% fat natural Greek yogurt**, and process for 2-3 minutes until thickened. Sieve 175g **self-raising flour** and 1 teaspoon **baking powder** into a bowl and stir in 100g **polenta**, 75g **caster sugar** and the grated zest of 2 **lemons**. Gently whisk in the apricot mixture until combined. Pour into the prepared tin and bake for 45-50 minutes, until a skewer inserted into the centre of the cake comes out clean. Let the cake cool in the tin completely then release carefully. Decorate with the pared zest of ½ **lemon**.

Chocolate fudge pops

makes 6   **prep time 5 minutes + freezing**

   3 2 2 per fudge pop

Put 250g **0% fat natural Greek yogurt**, 75ml **skimmed milk**, 3 tablespoons **cocoa powder** and 4 tablespoons **agave syrup** into a food processor or blender and blitz until combined. Divide between 6 x 75ml ice-lolly moulds, cover and freeze for 6 hours until solid.

Fro-yo bark

serves 6   **prep time 5 minutes + freezing**

   3 2 2 per serving

Line a 16cm x 26cm baking tin with baking paper. In a small bowl, mix together 250g **0% fat natural Greek yogurt**, 2 teaspoons **maple syrup** and 1 teaspoon **vanilla extract**. Spoon into the prepared baking tin and spread out evenly. Scatter over 80g sliced **mixed berries** (we used strawberries, blueberries and raspberries), 20g chopped fresh **pistachio kernels** and 20g chopped **dark chocolate**. Put in the freezer for 3-4 hours or until firm, then break into bite-size pieces to serve.

Harissa dip

serves 8   **prep time 5 minutes**

   0 0 0 per serving

Drain 200g **roasted red peppers in brine**, put into a mini food processor and blitz until smooth. Add 50g **0% fat natural Greek yogurt**, 1 teaspoon **harissa paste**, ¼ teaspoon finely chopped **garlic**, ¼ teaspoon **smoked paprika**, ¼ teaspoon **ground cumin** and the juice of ½ **lemon**, then blitz until smooth. Transfer to a bowl, season to taste and serve with a mixture of zero hero **vegetable crudités**.

Quorn & tofu

104 **Chilli tofu larb**

106 **Sticky tofu with broccoli**

108 **Quorn fajitas**

110 **Spaghetti with creamy herb sauce**

112 **Chilli & peanut tofu burgers with wedges**

114 **Quorn Thai green curry**

116 **Pea, leek & mint soup**

Mocha mousse pots

Mini lemon & passion fruit cheesecakes

Tofu & kimchi soup

Chilli tofu larb

serves 4   prep time 10 minutes + pressing   cook time 10 minutes

   per serving

Crumbled tofu is a great zero-hero substitute for the pork mince you'd usually find in this zesty, spicy Thai salad.

2 x 280g packs firm tofu

30g unsalted cashews

Calorie controlled cooking spray

2 teaspoons chopped fresh ginger

2 teaspoons chopped fresh garlic

2 red chillies, chopped

6 spring onions, trimmed and chopped

2 teaspoons light soy sauce

1 tablespoon maple syrup

Juice of 2 limes, plus wedges to serve

½ red onion, finely sliced

4 tablespoons chopped fresh Thai basil, plus extra leaves to serve

4 tablespoons chopped fresh coriander, plus extra leaves to serve

Handful mint leaves, to serve

1   Drain the tofu, wrap it in kitchen paper and put it on a plate. Top with another plate and settle a few full food tins on top. Leave for 10 minutes, then remove the kitchen paper and crumble the tofu into large pieces.

2   Toast the cashews in a dry frying pan for 2-3 minutes until golden, then remove from the pan and roughly chop and set aside.

3   Mist a large nonstick wok or frying pan with cooking spray and set over a medium heat. Stir-fry the ginger, garlic, chillies and spring onions for 1 minute, then add the tofu, soy sauce, maple syrup and lime juice. Stir-fry for 3-4 minutes, then stir in the red onion Thai basil and coriander.

4   Scatter over the toasted cashews, extra Thai basil, extra coriander and mint, then serve with the lime wedges on the side.

Cook's tip

Cook 200g 100% buckwheat soba noodles (dry weight) to pack instructions, then divide between plates and top with the larb.

Sticky tofu with broccoli

serves 4   prep time 10 minutes + pressing   cook time 20 minutes

   per serving

Firm tofu, cut into thick strips, makes a great addition to a stir-fry. Here, it's tossed in the wok with crunchy greens and coated in a sticky, Chinese-style chilli sauce.

2 x 280g packs firm tofu

320g Tenderstem broccoli

1 tablespoon vegetable oil

2 small red chillies, deseeded and sliced, plus extra slices to serve

2 garlic cloves, crushed

1 bunch choi sum, trimmed (or 2 pak choi, halved)

125ml vegetable stock, made with ½ stock cube

3 tablespoons light soy sauce

2 tablespoons Chinese rice wine

2 teaspoons chilli sauce

2 teaspoons cornflour

1 teaspoon sesame seeds, to serve

Large handful fresh coriander leaves, to serve

1   Drain the tofu, wrap it in kitchen paper and put it on a plate. Top with another plate and settle a few full food tins on top. Leave for 10 minutes, then remove the kitchen paper and cut the tofu into thick strips.

2   Meanwhile, blanch the broccoli in a pan of boiling water for 2-3 minutes, then drain and cool under cold running water.

3   Heat half the oil in a large nonstick wok or frying pan over a high heat. Cook the tofu, turning, for 3-4 minutes until golden all over. Remove from the wok and set aside.

4   Reduce the heat to medium, add the remaining oil and stir-fry the chilli and garlic for 1-2 minutes. Add the choi sum and broccoli and stir-fry for 2-3 minutes until the leaves have wilted.

5   Meanwhile, whisk together the vegetable stock, soy sauce, Chinese rice wine, chilli sauce and cornflour in a small bowl, then add to the wok and cook, stirring, for 2-3 minutes, until the sauce darkens and thickens.

6   Return the tofu to the pan and gently toss to coat. Cook for 2 minutes, or until the mixture is bubbling then serve garnished with the sesame seeds, coriander leaves and extra chilli slices.

Quorn fajitas

serves 4   prep time 10 minutes   cook time 15 minutes

   per serving

If you're vegetarian or simply trying to eat less meat, use Quorn instead of chicken or turkey in this family-favourite Mexican meal.

Calorie controlled cooking spray

2 x 350g packs Quorn pieces

1 red pepper, deseeded and sliced

1 yellow pepper, deseeded and sliced

1 red onion, sliced

2 teaspoons smoked paprika

2 teaspoons ground cumin

½ teaspoon chilli powder

4 WW White Wraps

4 tablespoons reduced-fat soured cream

50g WW Reduced Fat Grated Mature Cheese

Lime wedges, to serve

1 Preheat the oven to 200°C, fan 180°C, gas mark 6. Mist a large nonstick frying pan with cooking spray, and cook the Quorn pieces over a medium heat for 5 minutes or until golden. Stir in the vegetables and spices, season to taste and cook for a further 8-10 minutes, or until the vegetables are just softened and lightly golden.

2 Meanwhile, cover the wraps with kitchen foil and heat in the oven for 8 minutes.

3 Top each wrap with a quarter of the fajita mixture, soured cream and cheese, then roll up and serve with the lime wedges.

Why not try...
WW White Wraps – made with no artificial preservatives – are high-fibre, low-fat alternatives to regular wraps. Available in selected supermarkets.

Spaghetti with creamy herb sauce

serves 4   prep time 10 minutes   cook time 30 minutes

   per serving

A delicious free-from dish that uses silken tofu in place of dairy for a creamy, thick sauce, and lentil spaghetti instead of wheat-based pasta for a gluten-free base.

5 shallots, peeled and left whole

1 teaspoon olive oil

200g silken tofu

80g watercress

1 tablespoon fresh flat-leaf parsley, plus extra to garnish

Grated zest and juice of 1 lemon

200g WW Yellow Lentil Spaghetti

2 ripe plum tomatoes, diced, to serve

1   Preheat the oven to 200°C, fan 180°C, gas mark 6. Put the shallots onto a large sheet of kitchen foil and drizzle over the oil. Season, then wrap the foil into a parcel around the shallots, folding it at the edges to seal. Put the parcel onto a baking tray and bake for 30 minutes.

2   Put the tofu, watercress and parsley into a food processor or blender and process until smooth. Add the lemon juice and roasted shallots, and continue to pulse until smooth. Season to taste.

3   Meanwhile, bring a large pan of water to the boil and cook the spaghetti to pack instructions. Drain and stir together with the tofu sauce then serve seasoned to taste and garnished with the tomatoes, extra fresh parsley and the lemon zest.

Why not try...

WW Yellow Lentil Spaghetti, made from yellow lentil and brown rice flour, is completely gluten free and high in protein. Available at the WW online shop.

Chilli & peanut tofu burgers with wedges

serves 4   prep time 15 minutes + pressing   cook time 45 minutes

   per serving

Tofu makes excellent vegan burger patties as it carries flavours well – this one has a spicy satay kick and is served with crisp butternut squash wedges on the side.

600g butternut squash, cut into thin wedges

Calorie controlled cooking spray

1 teaspoon sesame seeds

280g firm tofu

2 tablespoons PBFit Peanut Butter Powder

1 red chilli, chopped

3 spring onions, trimmed and finely sliced

15g panko breadcrumbs

4 x 60g wholemeal burger buns, split

4 lettuce leaves

2 tomatoes, sliced

¼ cucumber, sliced

½ red onion, thinly sliced

FOR THE SATAY SAUCE

2 tablespoons PBFit Peanut Butter Powder

½ tablespoon light soy sauce

2 teaspoons agave syrup

1 tbsp lime juice

1   Preheat the oven to 200°C, fan 180°C, gas mark 6. Put the butternut squash on a baking tray, mist all over with cooking spray, then season and bake for 30 minutes. Scatter over the sesame seeds and cook for a further 15 minutes.

2   Meanwhile, drain the tofu, wrap it in kitchen paper and put it on a plate. Top with another plate and settle a few full food tins on top. Leave for 10 minutes, then remove the kitchen paper.

3   Combine the PBFit with 1½ tablespoons cold water until smooth, then put into a food processor with the tofu, chilli, spring onions and panko breadcrumbs. Pulse until combined, then form the mixture into 4 patties. Transfer to a baking tray lined with baking paper and bake alongside the wedges for the final 15 minutes of cooking time.

4   Make the satay sauce. In a small bowl, combine the PBFit with 1½ tablespoons cold water, then stir in the soy sauce, agave syrup and lime juice until combined.

5   Toast the burger buns and top the base of each with the lettuce, tomatoes, tofu patties, cucumber and red onion. Spoon over the satay sauce and sandwich with the bun tops. Serve with the butternut squash wedges on the side.

Cook's tip

To reduce the SmartPoints, omit the bun and serve the patties, salad and wedges with the satay sauce on the side.

Quorn Thai green curry

serves 4   prep time 20 minutes   cook time 30 minutes

  5 5 per serving

Making your own curry paste is not only satisfying, it also allows you to control the heat level. Increase or decrease the amount of chilli in this paste – the SmartPoints will stay the same.

Calorie controlled cooking spray

1 red pepper, deseeded and thinly sliced

150g chestnut mushrooms, sliced

400g tin reduced-fat coconut milk

250ml vegetable stock, made with 1 stock cube

280g pack frozen vegan Quorn pieces

200g mangetout

150g broccoli florets

2 tablespoons Thai basil leaves

Juice of 1 lime, plus wedges to serve

FOR THE CURRY PASTE

2 garlic cloves

4 shallots

2 teaspoons grated ginger

1 teaspoon lemongrass paste

2 green chillies, chopped

1 teaspoon ground cumin

½ teaspoon ground coriander

2 teaspoons light soy sauce

1 To make the curry paste, put all the paste ingredients into a mini food processor and blitz until smooth and combined.

2 Heat a large nonstick wok or frying pan over a high heat and mist with cooking spray. Stir-fry the pepper and mushrooms for 4-5 minutes, then add the curry paste and cook for 1-2 minutes. Pour in the coconut milk and vegetable stock, bring to a simmer and cook for 5 minutes.

3 Add the Quorn and cook, covered, for 10-12 minutes, then stir in the mangetout and broccoli and cook for a further 3-4 minutes.

4 Stir through the basil and lime juice then serve with the lime wedges on the side.

Cook's tip
Serve the curry with 75g cooked basmati rice per person.

Four variations... Silken tofu

The smooth, custard-like texture of silken tofu can be used to bring a thick, creaminess to everything from soups and dips to cheesecake fillings and chocolate desserts.

Pea, leek & mint soup

serves 4   prep time 20 minutes   cook time 15 minutes

4   0   0   per serving

Mist a nonstick pan with **calorie controlled cooking spray**. Cook 1 sliced **leek** and 1 chopped **onion** over a medium-low heat for 8-10 minutes, until tender. Add 500ml **vegetable stock** (made with 1 stock cube) and bring to the boil. Add 400g **frozen peas** and cook for 3-5 minutes until tender. Remove from the heat and add 340g **silken tofu**, a large handful each of **fresh mint** and **fresh flat-leaf parsley**, 2 tablespoons chopped **fresh chives**, and 1½ tablespoons **lemon juice**. Use a stick blender to blitz until smooth. Season to taste then ladle the soup into bowls and swirl ½ tablespoon **0% fat natural Greek yogurt** into each. Top with a handful of **pea shoots**, then season and serve.

Mini lemon & passion fruit cheesecakes

makes 8
prep time 15 minutes + chilling   cook time 15 minutes

5   4   4   per cheesecake

Mist 8 x WW 2 in 1 Mini Cake Moulds with **calorie controlled cooking spray**. Put 4 **low-fat digestives** (ensure vegan) into a mini food processor and blitz to a crumb. Transfer to a bowl and stir in 4 teaspoons melted **dairy-free spread**. Press the mixture over the bases of the moulds. Put onto a baking tray and chill in the freezer while you make the filling. Preheat the oven to 160°C, fan 140°C, gas mark 3. Put 300g drained **silken tofu** and 100g **vegan soft cheese** in a food processor. Blitz for 1 minute, then add 3 tablespoons **agave syrup** and blitz again. Whisk together the grated zest and juice of 1 **lemon**, the sieved pulp of 3 **passion fruit** and 1 tablespoon **cornflour**, then add this to the processor. Blend until smooth then divide between the moulds. Bake for 15 minutes, then turn off the oven, prop the door ajar and leave in the oven to cool completely. Cover and chill in the fridge until cold. Serve topped with passion fruit pulp, if you like.

Mocha mousse pots

makes 4   prep time 10 minutes + chilling cook time 5 minutes

5   4   4   per mousse pot

Break 25g **vegan dark chocolate** (we used Dr Oetker 54% Cocoa Solids) into pieces and put into a microwave-safe bowl. Cover and melt in the microwave, then set aside to cool. Drain the excess liquid from 300g room temperature **silken tofu** and pat dry with kitchen paper. Put into a food processor with 30g **cocoa powder**, 45ml cooled **espresso**, or strong black coffee, 2 tablespoons **agave syrup** and 1 teaspoon **vanilla extract**. Blend until smooth, then add the melted chocolate and pulse until combined. Divide the mixture between 4 small dessert glasses and pop into the fridge to chill until ready to serve. Grate or shave over 5g **vegan dark chocolate** before serving.

Tofu & kimchi soup

serves 4   prep time 15 minutes   cook time 20 minutes

3   3   3   per serving

Heat 1½ tablespoons **vegetable oil** in a large pan over a medium heat. Drain a 215g jar **kimchi** (ensure vegan), reserving the liquid, and add the kimchi to the pan. Stir in 1 small crushed **garlic** clove and cook, stirring frequently, for 5 minutes, until the kimchi is wilted and tender. Add the reserved **kimchi liquid** and 800ml water, then bring to the boil. Reduce to a simmer and add 225g **silken tofu**, cut into 2cm pieces. Trim and cut 4 **spring onions** into 2.5cm lengths, then add to the pan and simmer for 6-8 minutes. Add 100g **young leaf spinach** and cook for 2 minutes until wilted. Remove from the heat and stir in ¾ tablespoon **soy sauce**. Ladle into bowls then drizzle ¼ teaspoon **toasted sesame oil** over each bowl and serve garnished with sliced spring onions.

Meal plans

120 **Vegan**
122 **Family favourites**
124 **Quick & easy**

Vegan

serves 4

25 **20** **16** SmartPoints value

Plant-based eating doesn't get more delicious than this.

BREAKFAST
Apple & ginger overnight oats p20

4 **4** **1** Per serving

LUNCH
Tabbouleh with courgette & houmous p74

4 **4** **3** Per serving

DINNER
Quorn Thai green curry with basmati rice p114

9 **8** **8** Per serving

DESSERT
Lemon & passion fruit cheesecake p116

5 **4** **4** Per cheesecake

SNACK
Red lentil crisps p86

3 **0** **0** Per serving

Family favourites

serves 4

21 **16** **16** SmartPoints value

No need to cook separately! These recipes will keep everyone in the family happy.

BREAKFAST
Fruit salad with lime dressing p38

2 **2** **2** Per serving

LUNCH
Tuna & sweetcorn fritters p48

4 **2** **2** Per serving

DINNER
Frying pan turkey tacos p68

5 **3** **3** Per serving

DESSERT
Squidgy lemon polenta cake p100

7 **7** **7** Per serving

SNACK
Turkey & hoisin sausage rolls p68

3 **2** **2** Per sausage roll

Quick & easy

serves 4

(21) (15) (15) SmartPoints value

Busy days call for meals that come together in 30 minutes or under.

BREAKFAST
Turkish eggs p94

(4) (2) (2) Per serving

LUNCH
Salt & pepper prawns with mango salsa p54

(3) (2) (2) Per serving

DINNER
Quorn fajitas p108

(7) (5) (5) Per serving

DESSERT
Mocha mousse pots p116

(5) (4) (4) Per mousse pot

SNACK
Chickpea peanut butter cookies p82

(2) (2) (2) Per cookie

SmartPoints index

Green

0 SmartPoints

Harissa dip	100
Rosemary swede chips	44
Spiced squash & cauliflower fritters with red pepper salsa	26
Spice-roasted vegetables	44

1 SmartPoint

Cauliflower 'risotto'	32
Griddled lettuce with red pepper pesto & chimichurri	34
Red cabbage slaw	28
Spiced courgette soup	22
Thai yellow prawn curry	60
Tuna & courgette salad	48

2 SmartPoints

Butter bean fritters with yogurt & cucumber dip	76
Chickpea peanut butter cookies	82
Fruit salad with lime dressing	38
Roasted beetroot houmous	44
Satay vegetable noodles	36
Sea bass with black olive, tomato & basil salsa	58
Turkey patties with cauliflower & carrot salad	68

3 SmartPoints

Apple & kale slaw	20
Celeriac soup with ricotta toast	44
Chocolate fudge pops	100
Crispy buttermilk turkey	68
Fro-yo bark	100
Grilled chicken with mint chimichurri	62
Red lentil crisps	86
Roasted Tenderstem broccoli salad with cashew dressing	24
Salt & pepper prawns with mango salsa	54
Tofu & kimchi soup	116
Tuna melt	48
Turkey & hoisin sausage rolls	68

4 SmartPoints

Apple & ginger overnight oats	20
Braised chicken & lentils	56
Bulgur wheat tabbouleh with courgette & houmous	74
Frisée salad with bacon & egg	98
Green lentil & spinach polpette	86
Pea, leek & mint soup	116
Smoky pollock with spinach	52
Sticky tofu with broccoli	106
Toffee & walnut baked apples	20
Tuna & sweetcorn fritters	48
Turkish eggs	94

5 SmartPoints

Apple & oat crisp	20
Blueberry & coconut flapjacks	72
Butternut squash & kale curry	84
Chilli tofu larb	104
Frying pan turkey tacos	68
Herb & feta muffins	90
Mini lemon & passion fruit cheesecakes	116
Mocha mousse pots	116
Mushroom, spinach & lentil lasagne	78
Piri-piri roast chicken flatbreads	64
Quinoa with sticky harissa aubergine & pomegranate	80
Tuna & watercress salad	48

6 SmartPoints

Crispy chicken cutlets with tarragon butter vegetables	50
Coddled eggs	92
Plum & pistachio crumble	40
Quorn Thai green curry	114
Spaghetti with creamy herb sauce	110

7 SmartPoints

Chilli & peanut tofu burgers with wedges	112
Pineapple waffles	42
Quorn fajitas	108
Squidgy lemon polenta cake	100

8 SmartPoints

Miso-glazed salmon with braised leeks	66
Mushroom miso ramen	96
Puy lentil & edamame salad	86
Roast beetroot burgers	30

9 SmartPoints

Puy lentil bowl	86

Blue

0 SmartPoints

Braised chicken & lentils	56
Butter bean fritters with yogurt & cucumber dip	76
Harissa dip	100
Pea, leek & mint soup	116
Red lentil crisps	86
Rosemary swede chips	44
Spiced squash & cauliflower fritters with red pepper salsa	26
Spice-roasted vegetables	44
Tuna & courgette salad	48
Turkey patties with cauliflower & carrot salad	68

1 SmartPoint

Cauliflower 'risotto'	32
Green lentil & spinach polpette	86
Griddled lettuce with red pepper pesto & chimichurri	34
Grilled chicken with mint chimichurri	62
Puy lentil & edamame salad	86
Red cabbage slaw	28
Roasted beetroot houmous	44
Sea bass with black olive, tomato & basil salsa	58
Spiced courgette soup	22
Thai yellow prawn curry	60

2 SmartPoints

Butternut squash & kale curry	84
Chickpea peanut butter cookies	82
Chilli tofu larb	104
Chocolate fudge pops	100
Crispy buttermilk turkey	68
Frisée salad with bacon & egg	98
Fro-yo bark	100
Fruit salad with lime dressing	38
Salt & pepper prawns with mango salsa	54
Satay vegetable noodles	36
Sticky tofu with broccoli	106
Tuna & sweetcorn fritters	48
Turkey & hoisin sausage rolls	68
Turkish eggs	94

3 SmartPoints

Apple & kale slaw	20
Celeriac soup with ricotta toast	44
Coddled eggs	92
Frying pan turkey tacos	68

Purple

Miso-glazed salmon with braised leeks	66
Piri-piri roast chicken flatbreads	64
Roasted Tenderstem broccoli salad with cashew dressing	24
Smoky pollock with spinach	52
Tofu & kimchi soup	116
Tuna & watercress salad	48
Tuna melt	48

4 SmartPoints

Apple & ginger overnight oats	20
Bulgur wheat tabbouleh with courgette & houmous	74
Crispy chicken cutlets with tarragon butter vegetables	50
Mini lemon & passion fruit cheesecakes	116
Mocha mousse pots	116
Mushroom, spinach & lentil lasagne	78
Toffee & walnut baked apples	20

5 SmartPoints

Apple & oat crisp	20
Blueberry & coconut flapjacks	72
Herb & feta muffins	90
Puy lentil bowl	86
Quinoa with sticky harissa aubergine & pomegranate	80
Quorn fajitas	108
Quorn Thai green curry	114
Spaghetti with creamy herb sauce	110

6 SmartPoints

Chilli & peanut tofu burgers with wedges	112
Plum & pistachio crumble	40

7 SmartPoints

Mushroom miso ramen	96
Pineapple waffles	42
Roast beetroot burgers	30
Squidgy lemon polenta cake	100

0 SmartPoints

Braised chicken & lentils	56
Butter bean fritters with yogurt & cucumber dip	76
Harissa dip	100
Pea, leek & mint soup	116
Red lentil crisps	86
Rosemary swede chips	44
Spaghetti with creamy herb sauce	110
Spiced squash & cauliflower fritters with red pepper salsa	26
Spice-roasted vegetables	44
Tuna & courgette salad	48
Turkey patties with cauliflower & carrot salad	68

1 SmartPoint

Apple & ginger overnight oats	20
Cauliflower 'risotto'	32
Green lentil & spinach polpette	86
Griddled lettuce with red pepper pesto & chimichurri	34
Grilled chicken with mint chimichurri	62
Mushroom miso ramen	96
Puy lentil & edamame salad	86
Red cabbage slaw	28
Roasted beetroot houmous	44
Sea bass with black olive, tomato & basil salsa	58
Spiced courgette soup	22
Thai yellow prawn curry	60

2 SmartPoints

Butternut squash & kale curry	84
Chickpea peanut butter cookies	82
Chilli tofu larb	104
Chocolate fudge pops	100
Crispy buttermilk turkey	68
Frisée salad with bacon & egg	98
Fro-yo bark	100
Fruit salad with lime dressing	38
Mushroom, spinach & lentil lasagne	78
Puy lentil bowl	86
Quinoa with sticky harissa aubergine & pomegranate	80
Salt & pepper prawns with mango salsa	54
Satay vegetable noodles	36
Sticky tofu with broccoli	106
Tuna & sweetcorn fritters	48
Turkey & hoisin sausage rolls	68
Turkish eggs	94

3 SmartPoints

Apple & kale slaw	20
Blueberry & coconut flapjacks	72
Bulgur wheat tabbouleh with courgette & houmous	74
Celeriac soup with ricotta toast	44
Coddled eggs	92
Frying pan turkey tacos	68
Miso-glazed salmon with braised leeks	66
Piri-piri roast chicken flatbreads	64
Roasted Tenderstem broccoli salad with cashew dressing	24
Smoky pollock with spinach	52
Tofu & kimchi soup	116
Tuna & watercress salad	48
Tuna melt	48

4 SmartPoints

Apple & oat crisp	20
Crispy chicken cutlets with tarragon butter vegetables	50
Mini lemon & passion fruit cheesecakes	116
Mocha mousse pots	116
Plum & pistachio crumble	40
Toffee & walnut baked apples	20

5 SmartPoints

Herb & feta muffins	90
Quorn fajitas	108
Quorn Thai green curry	114

6 SmartPoints

Chilli & peanut tofu burgers with wedges	112
Roast beetroot burgers	30

7 SmartPoints

Pineapple waffles	42
Squidgy lemon polenta cake	100

Recipe index

APPLES
Apple & ginger overnight oats 20
Apple & kale slaw 20
Apple & oat crisp 20
Toffee & walnut baked apples 20
Apple & ginger overnight oats 20
Apple & kale slaw 20
Apple & oat crisp 20
AUBERGINES
Quinoa with sticky harissa
aubergine & pomegranate 80

BACON
Frisée salad with bacon & egg 98
BANANAS
Blueberry & coconut flapjacks 72
BEANS
Butter bean fritters with yogurt
& cucumber dip 76
Crispy chicken cutlets with
tarragon butter vegetables 50
Thai yellow prawn curry 60
Tuna & courgette salad 48
BEETROOT
Roast beetroot burgers 30
Roasted beetroot houmous 44
BLUEBERRIES
Blueberry & coconut flapjacks 72
Fruit salad with lime dressing 38
Blueberry & coconut flapjacks 72
Braised chicken & lentils 56
BROCCOLI
Puy lentil bowl 86
Quorn Thai green curry 114
Roasted Tenderstem broccoli
salad with cashew dressing 24
Sticky tofu with broccoli 106
BULGUR WHEAT
Bulgur wheat tabbouleh with
courgette & houmous 74
BURGERS
Chilli & peanut tofu burgers
with wedges 112
Roast beetroot burgers 30
Butter bean fritters with yogurt
& cucumber dip 76
BUTTERNUT SQUASH
Butternut squash & kale curry 84
Chilli & peanut tofu burgers
with wedges 112
Roasted Tenderstem broccoli
salad with cashew dressing 24
Spice-roasted vegetables 44
Spiced squash & cauliflower
fritters with red pepper salsa 26
Thai yellow prawn curry 60
Butternut squash & kale curry 84

CABBAGE
Apple & kale slaw 20

Crispy buttermilk turkey 68
Puy lentil & edamame salad 86
Puy lentil bowl 86
Red cabbage slaw 28
Satay vegetable noodles 36
Tuna & sweetcorn fritters 48
CAKES
Mini lemon & passion fruit
cheesecakes 116
Squidgy lemon polenta cake 100
CARROTS
Apple & kale slaw 20
Crispy buttermilk turkey 68
Crispy chicken cutlets with
tarragon butter vegetables 50
Puy lentil bowl 86
Red cabbage slaw 28
Satay vegetable noodles 36
Tuna & sweetcorn fritters 48
Turkey patties with cauliflower
& carrot salad 68
CAULIFLOWER
Cauliflower 'risotto' 32
Spiced squash & cauliflower
fritters with red pepper salsa 26
Thai yellow prawn curry 60
Turkey patties with cauliflower
& carrot salad 68
Cauliflower 'risotto' 32
CELERIAC
Celeriac soup with ricotta toast 44
CHEESE
Frying pan turkey tacos 68
Herb & feta muffins 90
Mushroom, spinach & lentil lasagne 78
Quorn fajitas 108
Tuna melt 48
CHERRIES
Fruit salad with lime dressing 38
CHICKEN
Braised chicken & lentils 56
Crispy chicken cutlets with
tarragon butter vegetables 50
Grilled chicken with mint chimichurri 62
Piri-piri roast chicken flatbreads 64
Chickpea peanut butter cookies 82
CHICKPEAS
Chickpea peanut butter cookies 82
Roasted beetroot houmous 44
Chilli & peanut tofu burgers
with wedges 112
Chilli tofu larb 104
CHIMICHURRI
Griddled lettuce with red
pepper pesto & chimichurri 34
Grilled chicken with mint chimichurri 62
CHOCOLATE
Apple & ginger overnight oats 20
Chickpea peanut butter cookies 82
Chocolate fudge pops 100

Fro-yo bark 100
Mocha mousse pots 116
Chocolate fudge pops 100
CHORIZO
Smoky pollock with spinach 52
COCONUT
Blueberry & coconut flapjacks 72
Pineapple waffles 42
Coddled eggs 92
COURGETTES
Bulgur wheat tabbouleh with
courgette & houmous 74
Satay vegetable noodles 36
Spiced courgette soup 22
Spice-roasted vegetables 44
Tuna & courgette salad 48
Crispy buttermilk turkey 68
Crispy chicken cutlets with
tarragon butter vegetables 50
CUCUMBER
Butter bean fritters with
yogurt & cucumber dip 76
Salt & pepper prawns with
mango salsa 54
CURRY
Butternut squash & kale curry 84
Spiced courgette soup 22
Quorn Thai green curry 114
Thai yellow prawn curry 60

EDAMAME
Puy lentil & edamame salad 86
EGGS
Coddled eggs 92
Frisée salad with bacon & egg 98
Mushroom miso ramen 96
Turkish eggs 94

FETA
Herb & feta muffins 90
FISH
Coddled eggs 92
Miso-glazed salmon with braised leeks 66
Sea bass with black olive,
tomato & basil salsa 58
Smoky pollock with spinach 52
Tuna & courgette salad 48
Tuna & sweetcorn fritters 48
Tuna & watercress salad 48
Tuna melt 48
FRESH BERRIES
Apple & ginger overnight oats 20
Blueberry & coconut flapjacks 72
Fro-yo bark 100
Fruit salad with lime dressing 38
Plum & pistachio crumble 40
Frisée salad with bacon & egg 98
FRITTERS
Butter bean fritters with
yogurt & cucumber dip 76

Spiced squash & cauliflower
fritters with red pepper salsa 26
Tuna & sweetcorn fritters 48
Fro-yo bark 100
Fruit salad with lime dressing 38
Frying pan turkey tacos 68

Green lentil & spinach polpette 86
Griddled lettuce with red
pepper pesto & chimichurri 34
Grilled chicken with mint chimichurri 62

HARISSA
Harissa dip 100
Quinoa with sticky harissa
aubergine & pomegranate 80
Turkey patties with cauliflower
& carrot salad 68
Harissa dip 100
Herb & feta muffins 90

KALE
Apple & kale slaw 20
Butternut squash & kale curry 84
Mushroom miso ramen 96
KIMCHI
Tofu & kimchi soup 116

LEEKS
Miso-glazed salmon with braised leeks 66
Pea, leek & mint soup 116
LEMONS
Mini lemon & passion fruit
cheesecakes 116
Squidgy lemon polenta cake 100
LENTIL PASTA
Mushroom, spinach & lentil lasagne 78
Spaghetti with creamy herb sauce 110
LENTILS
Braised chicken & lentils 56
Butternut squash & kale curry 84
Green lentil & spinach polpette 86
Puy lentil & edamame salad 86
Puy lentil bowl 86
Red lentil crisps 86
Roast beetroot burgers 30
LETTUCE
Frisée salad with bacon & egg 98
Griddled lettuce with red
pepper pesto & chimichurri 34
Piri-piri roast chicken flatbreads 64
Salt & pepper prawns with
mango salsa 54

MANGO
Salt & pepper prawns with mango salsa 54
Mini lemon & passion fruit cheesecakes 116
MISO
Miso-glazed salmon with braised leeks 66
Mushroom miso ramen 96

Miso-glazed salmon with
braised leeks 66
Mocha mousse pots 116
MUSHROOMS
Cauliflower 'risotto' 32
Mushroom miso ramen 96
Mushroom, spinach & lentil lasagne 78
Quorn Thai green curry 114
Roast beetroot burgers 30
Mushroom miso ramen 96
Mushroom, spinach & lentil lasagne 78

NOODLES
Mushroom miso ramen 96
NUTS
Apple & ginger overnight oats 20
Chickpea peanut butter cookies 82
Chilli & peanut tofu burgers
with wedges 112
Chilli tofu larb 104
Fro-yo bark 100
Fruit salad with lime dressing 38
Plum & pistachio crumble 40
Roasted Tenderstem broccoli
salad with cashew dressing 24
Satay vegetable noodles 36
Toffee & walnut baked apples 20

OATS
Apple & ginger overnight oats 20
Apple & oat crisp 20
Blueberry & coconut flapjacks 72
OLIVES
Sea bass with black olive,
tomato & basil salsa 58

PARSNIPS
Satay vegetable noodles 36
PASSION FRUIT
Mini lemon & passion
fruit cheesecakes 116
Pea, leek & mint soup 116
PEAS
Pea, leek & mint soup 116
Tuna & watercress salad 48
PEPPERS
Crispy buttermilk turkey 68
Frying pan turkey tacos 68
Griddled lettuce with red
pepper pesto & chimichurri 34
Harissa dip 100
Puy lentil & edamame salad 86
Quorn fajitas 108
Smoky pollock with spinach 52
Spiced squash & cauliflower
fritters with red pepper salsa 26
Spice-roasted vegetables 44
Tuna & sweetcorn fritters 48
PINEAPPLE
Pineapple waffles 42
Piri-piri roast chicken flatbreads 64
PLUMS
Plum & pistachio crumble 40
POMEGRANATE
Bulgur wheat tabbouleh with
courgette & houmous 74
Quinoa with sticky harissa
aubergine & pomegranate 80
PRAWNS
Salt & pepper prawns with mango salsa 54
Thai yellow prawn curry 60

Recipe index

Puy lentil & edamame salad 86
Puy lentil bowl 86

QUINOA
Quinoa with sticky harissa
aubergine & pomegranate 80
QUORN
Quorn fajitas 108
Quorn Thai green curry 114

Red cabbage slaw 28
Red lentil crisps 86
RICOTTA
Celeriac soup with ricotta toast 44
RISOTTO
Cauliflower 'risotto' 32
Roast beetroot burgers 30
Roasted beetroot houmous 44
Roasted Tenderstem broccoli
salad with cashew dressing 24
Rosemary swede chips 44

SALAD
Bulgur wheat tabbouleh with
courgette & houmous 74
Chilli tofu larb 104
Frisée salad with bacon & egg 98
Fruit salad with lime dressing 38
Puy lentil & edamame salad 86
Quinoa with sticky harissa
aubergine & pomegranate 80
Roasted Tenderstem broccoli
salad with cashew dressing 24
Salt & pepper prawns with
mango salsa 54
Turkey patties with
cauliflower & carrot salad 68
Tuna & courgette salad 48
Tuna & watercress salad 48

SALMON
Coddled eggs 92
Miso-glazed salmon with braised leeks 66
Salt & pepper prawns with mango salsa 54
SANDWICHES
Piri-piri roast chicken flatbreads 64
Tuna melt 48
Satay vegetable noodles 36
Sea bass with black olive,
tomato & basil salsa 58
SEEDS
Apple & kale slaw 20
Chilli & peanut tofu burgers
with wedges 112
Mushroom miso ramen 96
Puy lentil bowl 86
Red cabbage slaw 28
Sticky tofu with broccoli 106
Tuna & watercress salad 48
Turkey & hoisin sausage rolls 68
SLAW
Apple & kale slaw 20
Crispy buttermilk turkey 68
Red cabbage slaw 28
Tuna & sweetcorn fritters 48
Smoky pollock with spinach 52
SOUP
Celeriac soup with ricotta toast 44
Mushroom miso ramen 96
Pea, leek & mint soup 116
Spiced courgette soup 22
Tofu & kimchi soup 116
Spaghetti with creamy herb sauce 110
Spiced courgette soup 22
Spiced squash & cauliflower
fritters with red pepper salsa 26
Spice-roasted vegetables 44
SPINACH
Coddled eggs 92
Crispy chicken cutlets with
tarragon butter vegetables 50
Frying pan turkey tacos 68
Green lentil & spinach polpette 86
Mushroom, spinach & lentil lasagne 78
Sea bass with black olive,
tomato & basil salsa 58
Smoky pollock with spinach 52
Spiced courgette soup 22
Tofu & kimchi soup 116
Tuna & sweetcorn fritters 48
Squidgy lemon polenta cake 100
Sticky tofu with broccoli 106
STRAWBERRIES
Fruit salad with lime dressing 38
SWEDE
Rosemary swede chips 44
SWEET POTATO
Puy lentil bowl 86
Thai yellow prawn curry 60

Toffee & walnut baked apples 20
TOFU
Chilli & peanut tofu burgers
with wedges 112
Chilli tofu larb 104
Mocha mousse pots 116
Pea, leek & mint soup 116
Spaghetti with creamy herb sauce 110
Sticky tofu with broccoli 106
Tofu & kimchi soup 116
TOMATOES
Bulgur wheat tabbouleh
with courgette & houmous 74
Red cabbage slaw 28
Salt & pepper prawns with
mango salsa 54
Sea bass with black olive,
tomato & basil salsa 58
Smoky pollock with spinach 52
Spaghetti with creamy herb sauce 110
Thai yellow prawn curry 60
Tuna & courgette salad 48
TUNA
Tuna & courgette salad 48
Tuna & sweetcorn fritters 48
Tuna & watercress salad 48
Tuna melt 48
TURKEY
Crispy buttermilk turkey 68
Frying pan turkey tacos 68
Turkey & hoisin sausage rolls 68
Turkey patties with cauliflower
& carrot salad 68
Turkey & hoisin sausage rolls 68
Turkey patties with cauliflower
& carrot salad 68
Turkish eggs 94

WATERCRESS
Bulgur wheat tabbouleh
with courgette & houmous 74
Spaghetti with creamy herb sauce 110
Tuna & watercress salad 48

YOGURT
Butter bean fritters with
yogurt & cucumber dip 76
Chocolate fudge pops 100
Fro-yo bark 100
Green lentil & spinach polpette 86
Harissa dip 100
Pea, leek & mint soup 116
Piri-piri roast chicken flatbreads 64
Squidgy lemon polenta cake 100
Tuna & courgette salad 48
Tuna & watercress salad 48
Tuna melt 48
Turkish eggs 94